COOKING
FOR 2

TASTE OF HOME BOOKS • RDA ENTHUSIAST BRANDS, LLC • MILWAUKEE, WI

© 2020 RDA Enthusiast Brands, LLC.
1610 N. 2nd St., Suite 102, Milwaukee, WI 53212-3906
All rights reserved. Taste of Home is a registered
trademark of RDA Enthusiast Brands, LLC.

Visit us at tasteofhome.com for other
Taste of Home books and products.

ISBN: 978-1-61765-967-6
LOCC: 2020931537
Component Number: 116700100H

Executive Editor: Mark Hagen
Senior Art Director: Raeann Thompson
Assistant Art Director: Courtney Lovetere
Designer: Jazmin Delgado
Copy Editor: Sara Strauss

Cover:
Photographer: Jim Wieland
Set Stylist: Stacey Genaw
Food Stylist: Josh Rink

Pictured on front cover:
Lazy Lasagna, p. 76

Pictured on title page:
Grilled Jerk Shrimp Orzo Salad, p. 59

Pictured on back cover:
Air-Fryer Sweet & Sour Pork, p. 85
Grilled Pepper Jack Chicken Sandwiches, p. 61
Semisweet Chocolate Mousse, p. 103

Printed in USA
1 3 5 7 9 10 8 6 4 2

P. 57

P. 43

P. 86

P. 26

Love to cook but don't love all of the leftovers? Tired of wasting time, effort and money cooking large-yield dishes that eventually end up sitting in the fridge? Maybe you long for all of the comforting casseroles, snacks, soups and sweet treats that please a crowd but don't make sense for small households.

Whether you're an empty nester or a newlywed, or you're simply cooking for a pair, **Taste of Home Cooking for 2** has the answers! This all-new collection of small-serving recipes helps you whip up the mouthwatering favorites you crave in just the right quantities.

Each of the **167 incredible dishes** in this collection is sized right for one or two diners. From dips and spreads to entrees and desserts, the perfect dish is always at hand.

You'll also enjoy...

● An entire chapter dedicated to slow-cooker, Instant Pot and air-fryer dishes perfect for two.

● A complete set of nutrition facts with every recipe, and diabetic exchanges where applicable.

● Prep-and-cook timelines and step-by-step directions to help you plan meals effortlessly.

● Reader reviews and no-fuss tips from the pros at the *Taste of Home* Test Kitchen.

🍎 Best of all, an apple icon highlights the dishes that pare down calories, fat, sodium, carbohydrates and/or sugar. Now it's easier than ever to satisfy everyone at your table.

With full-color photos, heart-smart dinners, fast weeknight staples, holiday classics and so much more, **Taste of Home Cooking for 2** is your guide to quick-and-easy specialties sized right for your home.

CONTENTS

P. 62

P. 97

More ways to connect with us:

SHOPTASTEOFHOME.COM

SUNSHINE LIME RICKEY

This is my re-creation of the lime rickey sodas served at my favorite burger place. I even tried a version using my own homemade bitters.
—*Shelly Bevington, Hermiston, OR*

···

TAKES: 5 min. • **MAKES:** 2 servings

- 4   Tbsp. simple syrup
- 2   Tbsp. lime juice
- 2   Tbsp. orange juice
- 4   drops orange or lemon bitters
- 1   cup club soda, chilled
       Optional: Orange peel and fresh mint leaves

Fill 2 tall glasses three-fourths full with ice. Add half the simple syrup, lime juice, orange juice and bitters to each glass. Top each with ½ cup club soda; stir. Garnish as desired.

1 SERVING 130 cal., 0 fat (0 sat. fat), 0 chol., 25mg sod., 34g carb. (31g sugars, 0 fiber), 0 pro.

TEST KITCHEN TIP
···

This is a nonalcoholic lime rickey. Feel free to stir in a bit of gin if you'd like.

SNACKS & APPETIZERS
FOR TWO

Make tonight appetizer night! You won't have to fill the fridge with loads of leftovers. These special apps, snacks and drinks give you just the right amount of deliciousness.

RICH HOT
CHOCOLATE

RICH HOT CHOCOLATE

Each winter in early February, my friends and I gather for an outdoor show called Mittenfest. We skip the Bloody Marys and fill our thermoses with this hot cocoa instead.
—Gina Nistico, Denver, CO

....

TAKES: 15 min. • **MAKES:** 2 servings

- ⅔ cup heavy whipping cream
- 1 cup 2% milk
- 4 oz. dark chocolate candy bar, chopped
- 3 Tbsp. sugar
  Vanilla rum, optional
  Sweetened heavy whipping cream, whipped

In a small saucepan, heat heavy whipping cream, milk, chopped chocolate and sugar over medium heat just until mixture comes to a simmer, stirring constantly. Remove from heat; stir until smooth. If desired, add rum. Pour into 2 mugs; top with sweetened whipped cream.

1 CUP 653 cal., 49g fat (32g sat. fat), 107mg chol., 79mg sod., 60g carb. (56g sugars, 4g fiber), 9g pro.

BACON JALAPENO POPPERS

For an irresistible snack for two, try this spicy recipe. The bacon adds a smoky flavor to the traditional popper.
—Bernice Knutson, Danbury, IA

....

TAKES: 30 min. • **MAKES:** 2 servings

- 2 bacon strips, halved
- 4 tsp. cream cheese, softened
- 4 tsp. shredded Colby cheese
- 2 jalapeno peppers, halved lengthwise and seeded

1. In a small skillet, cook the bacon over medium heat until partially cooked but not crisp. Remove to paper towels to drain; keep warm.
2. Combine cheeses; spread into each pepper half. Wrap a piece of bacon around each pepper half. Place on a baking sheet.
3. Bake, uncovered, at 350° until bacon is crisp and the filling is heated through, 20-25 minutes.

2 POPPERS 160 cal., 15g fat (6g sat. fat), 31mg chol., 246mg sod., 1g carb. (1g sugars, 0 fiber), 5g pro.

GREEK PIZZA FOR TWO

GREEK PIZZA FOR TWO

Take your appetizers to the next level with a delicious flatbread pizza. It's fast, fresh and packed with a mouthwatering Mediterranean combo of artichokes, feta cheese, Greek olives and herbs.
—Cathi Schuett, Omaha, NE

....

TAKES: 20 min. • **MAKES:** 2 servings

- 1 Italian herb flatbread wrap
- 2½ tsp. Greek vinaigrette
- ¼ cup crumbled feta cheese
- 2 Tbsp. grated Parmesan cheese
- ¼ cup Greek olives, sliced
- ¼ cup water-packed artichoke hearts, rinsed, drained and chopped
- ¼ cup ready-to-use grilled chicken breast strips, chopped
  Dash each dried oregano, dried basil and pepper
- ½ cup shredded part-skim mozzarella cheese

1. Place wrap on an ungreased baking sheet; brush with vinaigrette. Layer with remaining ingredients.
2. Bake at 400° for 8-10 minutes or until cheese is melted.

½ PIZZA 295 cal., 17g fat (6g sat. fat), 39mg chol., 1062mg sod., 17g carb. (2g sugars, 2g fiber), 19g pro.

CARAMEL APPLE FLOAT

Who doesn't love the flavors of caramel, apples and vanilla ice cream together? If I'm feeling fancy, I drizzle extra caramel syrup around the inside of each glass right before adding the cider and ginger ale.
—*Cindy Reams, Philipsburg, PA*

TAKES: 10 min. • **MAKES:** 2 servings

- 1 cup chilled apple cider or unsweetened apple juice
- 1 cup chilled ginger ale or lemon-lime soda
- 1 cup vanilla ice cream
- 2 Tbsp. caramel sundae syrup Finely chopped peeled apple, optional

Divide cider and ginger ale between 2 glasses. Top each with ice cream; drizzle with caramel syrup. Add chopped apples if desired.

1 FLOAT 220 cal., 4g fat (2g sat. fat), 15mg chol., 102mg sod., 46g carb. (41g sugars, 0 fiber), 2g pro.

CHOCOLATE PEANUT BUTTER MUG CAKE

This is a delectable little cake in a coffee mug! Try it with almond milk, too.
—*Angela Lively, Conroe, TX*

PREP: 10 min. • **COOK:** 3 min.
MAKES: 1 serving

- 6 Tbsp. 2% milk
- 2 Tbsp. canola oil
- 6 Tbsp. all-purpose flour
- 3 Tbsp. sugar
- 3 Tbsp. quick-cooking oats
- ½ tsp. baking powder
- ¼ tsp. salt
- 2 Tbsp. semisweet chocolate chips
- 1 heaping Tbsp. creamy peanut butter

1. Spray a 12-oz. coffee mug with cooking spray. Combine milk and oil in mug. Add flour, sugar, oats, baking powder and salt; stir to combine. Add chocolate chips; dollop center with peanut butter.
2. Microwave on high until toothpick inserted in the center comes out clean, 2½ minutes. Serve immediately.

1 MUG CAKE 862 cal., 46g fat (9g sat. fat), 7mg chol., 945mg sod., 105g carb. (56g sugars, 5g fiber), 14g pro.

GRILLED SHRIMP WITH APRICOT SAUCE FOR TWO

Served fresh from the grill, bacon-wrapped shrimp skewers make a fabulous addition to a summer menu. These get a boost from a sweet-hot sauce.
—*Carole Resnick, Cleveland, OH*

TAKES: 20 min.
MAKES: 2 skewers (⅓ cup sauce)

- ¼ cup apricot preserves
- 1 Tbsp. apricot nectar
- ⅛ tsp. ground chipotle powder
- 6 uncooked large shrimp, peeled and deveined
- 3 slices Canadian bacon, halved

1. In a small bowl, combine the preserves, apricot nectar and chipotle powder. Chill until serving.
2. Thread shrimp and bacon onto 2 metal or soaked wooden skewers. Grill, covered, over medium heat for 3-4 minutes on each side or until the shrimp turn pink. Serve with sauce.

1 SKEWER WITH SAUCE 208 cal., 4g fat (1g sat. fat), 80mg chol., 613mg sod., 28g carb. (16g sugars, 0 fiber), 17g pro.

CHOCOLATE PEANUT
BUTTER MUG CAKE

SCALLOP KABOBS FOR TWO

CHOCOLATE PEANUT GRAHAMS

Cinnamon graham crackers make it easy to whip up a sweet snack anytime.
—Taste of Home *Test Kitchen*

....

PREP: 10 min. + chilling • **MAKES:** 8 cookies

- 4 whole cinnamon graham crackers, broken into quarters
- ¼ cup creamy peanut butter
- 1 cup semisweet chocolate chips
- 3 tsp. shortening

1. Spread half of the graham cracker quarters with peanut butter; top with remaining crackers.

2. In a microwave-safe bowl, melt the chocolate chips and shortening; stir until smooth. Dip graham cracker sandwiches into melted chocolate; place on a waxed paper-lined pan. Refrigerate until set.

2 COOKIES 376 cal., 24g fat (10g sat. fat), 0 chol., 164mg sod., 41g carb. (28g sugars, 4g fiber), 7g pro.

SCALLOP KABOBS FOR TWO

I'm always on the lookout for recipes that are lower in fat and heart-healthy. These kabobs fill the bill. I like to serve them with a fruit salad and light dessert.
—*Edie DeSpain, Logan, UT*

....

PREP: 25 min. + marinating
GRILL: 10 min.
MAKES: 2 servings

- 4½ tsp. lemon juice
- 4½ tsp. reduced-sodium soy sauce
- 1 Tbsp. canola oil
  Dash garlic powder
  Dash pepper
- ¾ lb. sea scallops
- 2 small green peppers, cut into 1½-in. pieces
- 1 cup cherry tomatoes

1. In a small bowl, combine the first 5 ingredients. Pour 2 Tbsp. marinade into a bowl or shallow dish. Add scallops and turn to coat. Cover and refrigerate for 20 minutes. Cover and refrigerate remaining marinade for basting.

2. Meanwhile, in a large saucepan, bring 3 cups water to a boil. Add green peppers; cover and boil for 2 minutes. Drain and immediately place peppers in ice water. Drain and pat dry.

3. Drain scallops, discarding marinade. On 4 metal or soaked wooden skewers, alternately thread the tomatoes, scallops and peppers.

4. On a greased grill rack, grill kabobs, covered, over medium heat, or broil 4 in. from the heat, for 3-5 minutes on each side or until the scallops are firm and opaque, basting occasionally with the reserved marinade.

2 KABOBS 235 cal., 7g fat (1g sat. fat), 56mg chol., 616mg sod., 12g carb. (4g sugars, 2g fiber), 30g pro.
DIABETIC EXCHANGES 4 lean meat, 2 vegetable, 1 fat.

ZIPPY TORTILLA CHIPS

If store-bought tortilla chips are too salty for you, give these homemade southwestern chips a try. You'll be pleasantly surprised at how quick and easy they are to make, and you're sure to get a spicy kick out of them!
—*Kim Sumrall, Aptos, CA*

TAKES: 20 min. • **MAKES:** 2 servings

- ½ tsp. brown sugar
- ¼ tsp. paprika
- ¼ tsp. garlic powder
- ¼ tsp. onion powder
- ¼ tsp. ground cumin
- ⅛ tsp. cayenne pepper
- 4 corn tortillas (6 in.)
  Cooking spray

1. In a small bowl, combine the first 6 ingredients. Stack the tortillas; cut into 6 wedges. Arrange in a single layer on a baking sheet coated with cooking spray.
2. Spritz the wedges with cooking spray; sprinkle with seasoning mixture. Bake at 375° for 9-10 minutes or until lightly browned. Cool for 5 minutes.
12 CHIPS 138 cal., 3g fat (0 sat. fat), 0 chol., 85mg sod., 26g carb. (2g sugars, 3g fiber), 3g pro.
DIABETIC EXCHANGES 1½ starch, ½ fat.

DEEP-FRIED ONIONS WITH DIPPING SAUCE

Enjoy this steakhouse appetizer right in your own home. We covered sweet onion wedges with a golden batter, fried them to perfection and added a zippy sauce.
—Taste of Home *Test Kitchen*

TAKES: 25 min. • **MAKES:** 2 servings

- 1 sweet onion
- ½ cup all-purpose flour
- 1 tsp. paprika
- ½ tsp. garlic powder
- ⅛ tsp. cayenne pepper
- ⅛ tsp. pepper

BEER BATTER
- ⅓ cup all-purpose flour
- 1 Tbsp. cornstarch
- ½ tsp. garlic powder
- ½ tsp. paprika
- ¼ tsp. salt
- ¼ tsp. pepper
- 7 Tbsp. beer or nonalcoholic beer
  Oil for deep-fat frying

DIPPING SAUCE
- ¼ cup sour cream
- 2 Tbsp. chili sauce
- ¼ tsp. ground cumin
- ⅛ tsp. cayenne pepper

1. Cut onion into 1-in. wedges and separate into pieces. In a shallow bowl, combine the flour, paprika, garlic powder, cayenne and pepper.
2. For batter, in another shallow bowl, combine the flour, cornstarch, garlic powder, paprika, salt and pepper. Stir in beer. Dip the onions into the flour mixture, then into batter and again into flour mixture.
3. In an electric skillet or deep-fat fryer, heat oil to 375°. Fry onions, a few at a time, for 1-2 minutes on each side or until golden brown. Drain on paper towels. In a small bowl, combine the sauce ingredients. Serve with onions.
1 SERVING 686 cal., 12g fat (7g sat. fat), 40mg chol., 1085mg sod., 119g carb. (20g sugars, 7g fiber), 16g pro.

SUGAR COOKIE S'MORES

SUGAR COOKIE S'MORES

Change up traditional s'mores by using sugar cookies and candy bars in place of the usual ingredients. It's a fun twist on a campfire classic.
—Taste of Home *Test Kitchen*

....

TAKES: 15 min. • **MAKES:** 4 servings

    8   fun-size Milky Way candy bars
    8   sugar cookies (3 in.)
    4   large marshmallows

1. Place 2 candy bars on each of 4 cookies; place on grill rack. Grill, uncovered, over medium-hot heat for 1-1½ minutes or until bottoms of cookies are browned
2. Meanwhile, using a long-handled fork, toast marshmallows 6 in. from the heat until golden brown, turning occasionally. Remove marshmallows from fork and place over candy bars; top with remaining cookies. Serve immediately.

1 SANDWICH COOKIE 271 cal., 10g fat (5g sat. fat), 13mg chol., 123mg sod., 43g carb. (31g sugars, 1g fiber), 3g pro.

TEST KITCHEN TIP

....

Feel free to get creative with this easy snack. Mix up the candy bars or try peanut butter or chocolate chip cookies.

ONION PITA PIZZA

ONION PITA PIZZA

With a mild blue cheese and onion flavor and a crispy pita crust, this hits the spot with your favorite summer beverage.
—*Mary Lou Wayman, Salt Lake City, UT*

....

PREP: 25 min. • **BAKE:** 15 min.
MAKES: 2 servings

- 1 large onion, thinly sliced
- 1 Tbsp. butter
- 1 pita bread (6 in.)
- ⅔ cup 1% cottage cheese
- 2 Tbsp. crumbled blue cheese
- 2 Tbsp. chopped walnuts, toasted

1. In a small skillet, cook onion in butter over low heat for 20-25 minutes or until golden, stirring occasionally. Meanwhile, place pita bread on an ungreased baking sheet. Bake at 350° for 8-10 minutes or until lightly browned.

2. In a food processor, combine cottage cheese and blue cheese; cover and process until blended. Spread over pita bread; top with onion. Sprinkle with walnuts. Bake 3-5 minutes longer or until heated through. Cut into wedges.

½ PIZZA 293 cal., 14g fat (6g sat. fat), 25mg chol., 645mg sod., 26g carb. (7g sugars, 2g fiber), 17g pro.

SIMPLE SWISS CHEESE FONDUE

My friend's mother used to serve us her special fondue. Each time I make it, it brings back fond memories. Happy dipping!
—*Tracy Lawson, Plain City, UT*

....

TAKES: 20 min. • **MAKES:** ⅔ cup

- 1 cup shredded Swiss cheese
- 1 Tbsp. all-purpose flour
- ⅛ tsp. ground mustard
  Dash ground nutmeg
- ¼ cup half-and-half cream
- ¼ cup beer or nonalcoholic beer
- 4 slices French bread (1 in. thick), cut into 1-in. cubes

1. In a small bowl, combine the cheese, flour, mustard and nutmeg. In a small saucepan, heat the cream and beer over medium heat until bubbles form around sides of saucepan. Stir in cheese mixture. Bring just to a gentle boil; cook and stir for 1-2 minutes or until combined and smooth.

2. Transfer to a small fondue pot and keep warm. Serve with bread cubes.

⅓ CUP (WITHOUT BREAD) 280 cal., 20g fat (12g sat. fat), 65mg chol., 117mg sod., 6g carb. (2g sugars, 0 fiber), 16g pro.

DECADENT CHOCOLATE SHAKES

These rich and creamy shakes will make you feel as if you're sitting in a 1950s soda fountain. Update with a fun, over-the-top garnish like skewered doughnut holes or chocolate-dipped cookies.
—Taste of Home *Test Kitchen*

TAKES: 10 min. • **MAKES:** 2 cups

- ¾ cup 2% milk
- 1½ cups chocolate ice cream
- ¼ cup creamy peanut butter
- 2 Tbsp. chocolate syrup
  Optional toppings: Sweetened whipped cream; miniature peanut butter cups, quartered; and additional chocolate syrup

In a blender, combine the milk, ice cream, peanut butter and syrup; cover and process until smooth. If desired, garnish with whipped cream, peanut butter cups and additional chocolate syrup.

1 CUP 501 cal., 29g fat (11g sat. fat), 41mg chol., 262mg sod., 51g carb. (43g sugars, 3g fiber), 14g pro.

"Chocolate and peanut butter are two of my favorite flavors. This is definitely a shake I will make again!"
REMENIC, TASTEOFHOME.COM

DECADENT CHOCOLATE SHAKES

SANTA FE DEVILED EGGS

My deviled eggs have a zippy southwestern flair. The smoky, spicy flavor is always a hit with my husband.
—*Patricia Harmon, Baden, PA*

TAKES: 15 min. • **MAKES:** 2 servings

- 2 hard-boiled large eggs
- 1 Tbsp. mayonnaise
- 1 Tbsp. canned chopped green chiles
- ½ tsp. chipotle pepper in adobo sauce
- ⅛ tsp. garlic salt
- 4 tsp. salsa
- 1 pitted ripe olive, sliced
- 1½ tsp. thinly sliced green onion

1. Cut eggs in half lengthwise. Remove yolks; set whites aside. In a small bowl, mash yolks. Stir in the mayonnaise, chiles, chipotle pepper and garlic salt. Stuff or pipe into egg whites.
2. Top each with salsa, an olive slice and onion slices. Refrigerate until serving.
2 FILLED EGG HALVES 136 cal., 11g fat (2g sat. fat), 215mg chol., 298mg sod., 2g carb. (1g sugars, 0 fiber), 6g pro.

**SAUSAGE
CHEESE BALLS**

CHOCOLATE CINNAMON TOAST

Looking for a sweet snack or dessert? Toast cinnamon bread in a skillet and top it with chocolate and fresh fruit. Add a dollop of whipped cream for extra indulgence.
—*Jeanne Ambrose, Milwaukee, WI*

....

TAKES: 10 min. • **MAKES:** 1 serving

- 1 slice cinnamon bread
- 1 tsp. butter, softened
- 2 Tbsp. 60% cacao bittersweet chocolate baking chips
  Optional: Sliced banana and strawberries

Spread both sides of bread with butter. In a small skillet, toast bread over medium-high heat 2-3 minutes on each side, topping with chocolate chips after turning. Remove from heat; spread melted chocolate evenly over toast. If desired, top with fruit.

1 SLICE 235 cal., 13g fat (8g sat. fat), 10mg chol., 131mg sod., 29g carb. (19g sugars, 3g fiber), 4g pro.

REFRESHING TOMATO BRUSCHETTA

This recipe is especially yummy with sun-warmed tomatoes and basil fresh from the garden. My husband and I love this so much, we'll make a meal of it alone!
—*Greta Igl, Menomonee Falls, WI*

....

TAKES: 20 min. • **MAKES:** 2 servings

- 3 tsp. olive oil, divided
- 4 slices French bread (½ in. thick)
- 1 garlic clove, cut in half lengthwise
- ¾ cup chopped seeded tomato
- 1 Tbsp. minced fresh basil
- ½ tsp. minced fresh parsley
- ½ tsp. red wine vinegar
- ⅛ tsp. salt
- ⅛ tsp. pepper

1. Brush ½ tsp. oil over 1 side of each slice of bread; place the bread on a baking sheet. Bake at 350° for 5-7 minutes or until lightly browned. Rub cut side of garlic over bread.
2. Meanwhile, in a small bowl, combine the tomato, basil, parsley, vinegar, salt, pepper and remaining 1 tsp. oil. Spoon onto bread; serve immediately.

2 SLICES 155 cal., 8g fat (1g sat. fat), 0 chol., 327mg sod., 19g carb. (2g sugars, 2g fiber), 3g pro.
DIABETIC EXCHANGES 1½ fat, 1 starch.

SAUSAGE CHEESE BALLS

These bite-sized meatballs are a favorite of mine. Feel free to swap in a different cheese for the cheddar or to serve the balls with Dijon mustard instead of the barbecue and sweet-and-sour sauces.
—*Anna Damon, Bozeman, MT*

....

TAKES: 30 min. • **MAKES:** 1 dozen

- ½ cup shredded cheddar cheese
- 3 Tbsp. biscuit/baking mix
- 1 Tbsp. finely chopped onion
- 1 Tbsp. finely chopped celery
- ⅛ tsp. garlic powder
- ⅛ tsp. pepper
- ¼ lb. bulk pork sausage
  Optional: Sweet-and-sour and barbecue sauces

1. In a small bowl, combine the first 6 ingredients. Crumble sausage over mixture and mix well. Shape into 1-in. balls.
2. Place in a shallow baking pan coated with cooking spray. Bake, uncovered, at 375° for 12-15 minutes or until no longer pink. Drain on paper towels. Serve with sauces if desired.

6 PIECES 265 cal., 18g fat (8g sat. fat), 60mg chol., 685mg sod., 10g carb. (2g sugars, 0 fiber), 18g pro.›

CHOCOLATE
CINNAMON TOAST

COUSCOUS TABBOULEH WITH FRESH MINT & FETA

Using couscous instead of bulgur for tabbouleh really speeds up the process of making this colorful salad. Other quick-cooking grains, such as barley and quinoa, also work well.
—*Elodie Rosinovsky, Brighton, MA*

TAKES: 20 min. • **MAKES:** 3 servings

- ¾ cup water
- ½ cup uncooked couscous
- 1 can (15 oz.) garbanzo beans or chickpeas, rinsed and drained
- 1 large tomato, chopped
- ½ English cucumber, halved and thinly sliced
- 3 Tbsp. lemon juice
- 2 tsp. grated lemon zest
- 2 tsp. olive oil
- 2 tsp. minced fresh mint
- 2 tsp. minced fresh parsley
- ¼ tsp. salt
- ⅛ tsp. pepper
- ¾ cup crumbled feta cheese
  Lemon wedges, optional

1. In a small saucepan, bring water to a boil. Stir in couscous. Remove from the heat; cover and let stand for 5-8 minutes or until water is absorbed. Fluff with a fork.

2. In a large bowl, combine the beans, tomato and cucumber. In a small bowl, whisk the lemon juice, lemon zest, oil and seasonings. Drizzle over the bean mixture. Add couscous; toss to combine. Serve immediately or refrigerate until chilled. Sprinkle with cheese. If desired, serve with lemon wedges.

1⅔ CUPS 362 cal., 11g fat (3g sat. fat), 15mg chol., 657mg sod., 52g carb. (7g sugars, 9g fiber), 15g pro.

TEST KITCHEN TIP

Make this refreshing main dish salad gluten free by replacing the couscous with about 1½ cups cooked quinoa.

SALADS
FOR TWO

Keep the big bowls in the cupboard—
no supersize salads here! These reduced
recipes make perfect ways to toss together
a refreshing side or even an entree.

HEARTY ASIAN LETTUCE SALAD

HEARTY ASIAN LETTUCE SALAD

It may sound nutty, but this meatless version of a popular restaurant salad packs in 13 grams of protein per serving and just bursts with juicy flavor.
—Taste of Home *Test Kitchen*

TAKES: 20 min. • **MAKES:** 2 servings

- 1 cup ready-to-serve brown rice
- 1 cup frozen shelled edamame
- 3 cups spring mix salad greens
- ¼ cup reduced-fat sesame ginger salad dressing
- 1 medium navel orange, peeled and sectioned
- 4 radishes, sliced
- 2 Tbsp. sliced almonds, toasted

1. Prepare rice and edamame according to package directions.
2. In a large bowl, combine salad greens, rice and edamame. Drizzle with the salad dressing and toss to coat. Divide the salad mixture between 2 plates; top with orange segments, radishes and almonds.
1 SERVING 329 cal., 10g fat (1g sat. fat), 0 chol., 430mg sod., 44g carb. (12g sugars, 7g fiber), 13g pro.

TEST KITCHEN TIP

This is a perfect main dish salad for cold weather, when gardens are still under a layer of frost. For a heartier version, add sauteed shrimp or even leftover rotisserie chicken.

SUNFLOWER BROCCOLI SALAD

SUNFLOWER BROCCOLI SALAD

Broccoli can be delectable! When I toss it with bacon, onion, raisins, sunflower seeds and dressing, we nearly lick the bowl clean.
—Marilyn Newcomer, Sun City, CA

PREP: 20 min. + chilling • **MAKES:** 2 servings

- 2 cups fresh broccoli florets
- 2 bacon strips, cooked and crumbled
- 1 green onion, chopped
- 3 Tbsp. raisins
- 1 Tbsp. sunflower kernels

DRESSING
- ⅓ cup mayonnaise
- 4 tsp. sugar
- 2 tsp. white vinegar

In a bowl, combine broccoli, bacon, onion, raisins and kernels. In a small bowl, combine the dressing ingredients; stir until smooth. Pour over broccoli mixture and toss gently. Cover and refrigerate for at least 2 hours before serving, stirring occasionally.
1 CUP 290 cal., 19g fat (3g sat. fat), 19mg chol., 464mg sod., 27g carb. (21g sugars, 3g fiber), 6g pro.

KIDNEY BEAN SALAD

My daughter's friend made this as a side dish, but it's hearty enough to enjoy as a light lunch or even a dinner entree.
—Zelma McKinney, Amarillo, TX

TAKES: 15 min. • **MAKES:** 2 servings

- 1 can (16 oz.) kidney beans, rinsed and drained
- 2 hard-boiled large eggs, chopped
- ½ cup sliced celery
- 1 small onion, chopped
- ¼ cup mayonnaise
- ¼ cup dill pickle relish
- ½ tsp. pepper
- ¼ tsp. salt
  Leaf lettuce, optional

In a bowl, combine all of the ingredients except the lettuce; stir until coated. Refrigerate until serving. Serve in a lettuce-lined bowl if desired.
1½ CUPS 532 cal., 28g fat (5g sat. fat), 222mg chol., 1227mg sod., 51g carb. (16g sugars, 13g fiber), 21g pro.

TURKEY SPINACH SALAD WITH MAPLE DRESSING

My husband and I like to go hiking in New England. Vermont maple syrup is so good, and we always bring some home. I created a recipe that reminds us of those vacations.
—*Jessica Gerschitz, Jericho, NY*

TAKES: 15 min. • **MAKES:** 2 servings

- 6 oz. fresh baby spinach (about 7 cups)
- ¼ lb. sliced deli smoked turkey, cut into strips
- ⅔ cup sliced baby portobello mushrooms
- ⅓ cup sliced red onion
- 1 hard-boiled large egg, chopped
- ¼ cup walnut halves
- ¼ cup dried cranberries
- 4½ tsp. olive oil
- 1½ tsp. red wine vinegar
- 1 small garlic clove, minced
- 1½ tsp. finely chopped shallot
- 1½ tsp. Dijon mustard
- 1 Tbsp. maple syrup

In a large salad bowl, combine the first 7 ingredients. In a small bowl, whisk the remaining ingredients. Drizzle over salad; toss to coat.
3½ CUPS 387 cal., 22g fat (3g sat. fat), 126mg chol., 617mg sod., 30g carb. (18g sugars, 4g fiber), 21g pro.

NUTTY GREEN SALAD

A light curry-orange dressing is the star of this crunchy, colorful dish.
—*Barbara Robbins, Chandler, AZ*

TAKES: 10 min. • **MAKES:** 2 servings

- 2 cups spring mix salad greens
- 1 medium carrot, shredded
- 8 pecan halves, chopped

CURRY CITRUS DRESSING
- 2 Tbsp. orange juice
- 2 tsp. canola oil
- 1 tsp. balsamic vinegar
- ¼ tsp. curry powder
  Dash salt
  Dash pepper

In a bowl, combine the salad greens, carrot and pecans. In a jar with a tight-fitting lid, combine the dressing ingredients; shake well. Drizzle over salad and toss to coat.
1 SERVING 112 cal., 9g fat (1g sat. fat), 0 chol., 99mg sod., 8g carb. (4g sugars, 3g fiber), 2g pro.
DIABETIC EXCHANGES 1½ vegetable, 1½ fat.

TURKEY SPINACH SALAD WITH MAPLE DRESSING

WHITE BEAN
ARUGULA SALAD

🍎 WATERMELON–BLUEBERRY SALAD

Toss fresh berries and melon with a blend of honey, lemon juice and mint. People love the unusual but refreshing combination of flavors, especially on hot summer evenings.
—*Jenni Sharp, Milwaukee, WI*

....

TAKES: 5 min. • **MAKES:** 2 servings

1	Tbsp. honey
¾	tsp. lemon juice
½	tsp. minced fresh mint
1	cup seeded chopped watermelon
½	cup fresh blueberries

In a small bowl, combine honey, lemon juice and mint. Add watermelon and blueberries; toss gently to coat. Chill until serving.
¾ CUP 78 cal., 0 fat (0 sat. fat), 0 chol., 2mg sod., 20g carb. (17g sugars, 1g fiber), 1g pro.
DIABETIC EXCHANGES 1 fruit, ½ starch.

WHITE BEAN ARUGULA SALAD

My red, white and green ingredients were inspired by the Italian flag. Shaved Parmesan is the perfect finishing touch.
—*Malia Estes, Allston, MA*

....

TAKES: 30 min. • **MAKES:** 4 servings

4	slices pancetta, chopped
2	Tbsp. olive oil
¼	cup chopped sweet onion
⅔	cup cherry tomatoes, halved
1	tsp. minced fresh rosemary or ¼ tsp. dried rosemary, crushed
¼	tsp. salt
¼	tsp. pepper
2	cans (15 oz. each) cannellini beans, rinsed and drained
3	Tbsp. red wine vinegar
4	fresh basil leaves, thinly sliced
2	cups torn fresh arugula or baby spinach
¼	cup shaved Parmesan cheese

1. In a small skillet, cook the pancetta over medium heat until crisp, stirring occasionally. Remove with a slotted spoon; drain on paper towels.
2. In same pan, heat oil and pancetta drippings over medium heat. Add onion; cook and stir 1-2 minutes or until tender. Add tomatoes, rosemary, salt and pepper; cook 2-3 minutes longer or until tomatoes are softened. Cool slightly.
3. In a large bowl, combine beans, tomato mixture, pancetta, vinegar and basil. Add arugula and cheese; toss to coat.
1 CUP 340 cal., 16g fat (4g sat. fat), 23mg chol., 915mg sod., 33g carb. (1g sugars, 9g fiber), 15g pro.

GARLIC RANCH POTATO SALAD

As my taste tester, my husband usually tells me to add something to spice up a dish. This was the first recipe I experimented with that didn't need anything else. The hint of garlic in the dressing and the fresh herbs bring just the right flavor to the savory salad.
—*Amy Kowal, Pittsburgh, PA*

PREP: 30 min. + chilling • **MAKES:** 2 servings

- ¾ lb. medium red potatoes, cubed
- ¼ tsp. salt
- ⅛ tsp. pepper
- ½ cup garlic ranch salad dressing
- ¼ cup chopped sweet red pepper
- 2 Tbsp. grated Parmesan cheese
- 1 Tbsp. minced fresh basil or 1 tsp. dried basil
- ½ tsp. minced fresh rosemary or ⅛ tsp. dried rosemary, crushed

1. Place potatoes in a saucepan; cover with water. Bring to a boil. Reduce heat; cover and cook for 8-10 minutes or until tender. Drain and cool. Transfer to a large bowl; sprinkle with salt and pepper.
2. In a small bowl, whisk the remaining ingredients; pour over potatoes and toss to coat. Cover and refrigerate for at least 2 hours before serving.
1 CUP 450 cal., 34g fat (6g sat. fat), 14mg chol., 863mg sod., 33g carb. (4g sugars, 3g fiber), 5g pro.

CHOCOLATE PEAR & CHERRY SALAD

It's fun to come up with new ways to use the ingredients we love. I developed a chocolate vinaigrette, knowing how well it would work with stone fruit, the peppery bite of arugula and the deep acidic sweetness of balsamic. There are tons of other options that can go with the vinaigrette, so feel free to play!
—*Ryan Christie, Pacheco, CA*

PREP: 25 min. + chilling • **BAKE:** 15 min.
MAKES: 2 servings

- ¾ cup cut French green beans (*haricots verts*)
- 3 Tbsp. olive oil, divided
- ⅛ tsp. salt
- ⅛ tsp. pepper
- ¼ cup balsamic vinegar
- 1 oz. dark chocolate candy bar, chopped
- 1 Tbsp. red wine vinegar
- 4 cups fresh arugula
- 1 medium pear, peeled and cut into ½-in. cubes
- ½ cup frozen pitted sweet cherries, thawed and halved
- ¼ cup dried cranberries
- 3 Tbsp. coarsely chopped pecans
- 1 Tbsp. minced dried apricots
- 2 tsp. thinly sliced fresh mint leaves

1. Heat oven to 350°. In an 8-in. square baking dish, toss beans with 1 Tbsp. olive oil, salt and pepper. Roast until tender, 12-15 minutes. Remove from oven. Toss with balsamic vinegar; refrigerate, covered, 1½-2 hours.
2. Meanwhile, in a microwave, melt the chocolate; stir until smooth. Pulse melted chocolate, red wine vinegar and remaining olive oil in a blender until smooth.
3. Divide arugula evenly between 2 salad bowls. Drizzle with the chocolate mixture. Top with pears, cherries, cranberries and beans; sprinkle with pecans, apricots and mint leaves.
1 SERVING 511 cal., 33g fat (6g sat. fat), 2mg chol., 166mg sod., 62g carb. (47g sugars, 8g fiber), 4g pro.

TEST KITCHEN TIP

Adjust the amount of dressing to the size of salad you wish to make; a little goes a long way with this one! Dried currants make an awesome substitution for the dried cranberries.

THAI SHRIMP SALAD

THAI SHRIMP SALAD

Love Thai food? This is a deliciously different grilling idea that combines shrimp, a lean source of protein, with the low-calorie crunch of cucumber and onion.
—*Annette Traverso, San Rafael, CA*

PREP: 25 min. • GRILL: 10 min.
MAKES: 2 servings

2	Tbsp. lime juice
1	Tbsp. sesame oil
1	Tbsp. reduced-sodium soy sauce
1½	tsp. sesame seeds, toasted
1½	tsp. minced fresh mint
1½	tsp. minced fresh cilantro
	Dash crushed red pepper flakes
½	lb. uncooked large shrimp, peeled and deveined
⅛	tsp. salt
⅛	tsp. pepper
½	large sweet onion, sliced
½	medium cucumber, peeled and sliced
2	cups torn leaf lettuce

1. In a large bowl, combine the first 7 ingredients; set aside. Sprinkle shrimp with salt and pepper; thread onto 2 metal or soaked wooden skewers.
2. Place skewers on an oiled grill rack. Grill, covered, over medium heat or broil 4 in. from the heat until shrimp turn pink, 2-4 minutes.
3. Stir the dressing; add the shrimp, onion and cucumber. Toss to coat. Divide lettuce among 2 salad plates; top with the shrimp mixture and serve immediately.
1 SERVING 212 cal., 9g fat (1g sat. fat), 138mg chol., 614mg sod., 11g carb. (4g sugars, 3g fiber), 21g pro.
DIABETIC EXCHANGES 3 lean meat, 2 vegetable, 1½ fat.

CLASSIC MACARONI SALAD

CLASSIC MACARONI SALAD

You can't go wrong with this time-tested winner. Here it is pared down for two.
—*Carma Blosser, Livermore, CO*

....

TAKES: 15 min. • **MAKES:** 2 servings

- ¾ cup uncooked elbow macaroni
- ⅓ cup frozen peas
- ⅓ cup cubed cheddar cheese
- 3 Tbsp. chopped celery
- ¼ cup mayonnaise
- 1 tsp. finely chopped onion
- 1 tsp. finely chopped green pepper
- 1 tsp. diced pimientos
- ⅛ tsp. salt

Cook macaroni according to package directions, adding peas during the last 2 minutes of cooking. Drain and rinse in cold water. In a small bowl, combine the remaining ingredients. Stir in macaroni and peas. Chill until serving.

1 CUP 276 cal., 15g fat (4g sat. fat), 24mg chol., 544mg sod., 28g carb. (4g sugars, 2g fiber), 10g pro.

RHUBARB-STRAWBERRY GELATIN MOLDS

A neighbor with a very large, beautiful rhubarb and strawberry patch gave me one of her favorite recipes. It quickly became one of mine as well!
—*Janice Wiebelt, Hartville, OH*

....

PREP: 15 min. + chilling • **MAKES:** 2 servings

- 1 cup diced fresh or frozen rhubarb
- ¼ cup water
- 1 Tbsp. sugar
- 3 Tbsp. plus 1 tsp. strawberry gelatin
- ¼ cup sliced fresh strawberries
- ¼ cup orange juice
- ¼ tsp. grated orange zest
  Whipped cream, optional

1. In a small saucepan over medium heat, bring the rhubarb, water and sugar to a boil. Reduce the heat; simmer, uncovered, for 3-5 minutes or until the rhubarb is tender. Remove from the heat; stir in gelatin until dissolved. Add the strawberries, orange juice and zest.

2. Divide between two 4-in. mini fluted pans coated with cooking spray; refrigerate for 4 hours or until firm. Just before serving, invert molds onto serving plates; garnish with whipped cream if desired.

1 SERVING 143 cal., 0 fat (0 sat. fat), 0 chol., 56mg sod., 34g carb. (31g sugars, 2g fiber), 3g pro.
DIABETIC EXCHANGES 1½ starch, ½ fruit.

TEST KITCHEN TIP

....

Running short on time? Chop the strawberries instead of slicing them, and leave out the orange zest.

MEATLESS TACO SALAD

This colorful entree combines popular taco ingredients—minus the ground beef. And you won't miss the meat at all! I top each serving with a creamy guacamole dressing, crunchy corn chips and cheese.
—*Kimberly Dray, Pflugerville, TX*

TAKES: 20 min. • **MAKES:** 2 servings

- ⅓ cup guacamole
- ¼ cup sour cream
- 1 Tbsp. prepared Italian salad dressing
- 1 Tbsp. chopped green onions
- 2 Tbsp. chopped green pepper
- ¼ tsp. pepper
- ¼ tsp. chili powder
- 3 cups shredded lettuce
- 8 cherry tomatoes, halved
- ½ cup canned kidney beans, rinsed and drained
- ¼ cup sliced ripe olives
- ½ cup crushed corn chips
- ½ cup shredded cheddar cheese

In a small bowl, combine the first 7 ingredients; set aside. In a large bowl, combine the lettuce, tomatoes, beans and olives. Arrange lettuce mixture on 2 serving plates; top with the guacamole mixture. Sprinkle with corn chips and cheese.

1 SERVING 486 cal., 33g fat (12g sat. fat), 35mg chol., 849mg sod., 34g carb. (7g sugars, 9g fiber), 16g pro.

MEATLESS TACO SALAD

SPECIAL FRUIT SALAD

Brighten any day with this six-fruit salad featuring a drizzle of citrusy flavor.
—*Alice Orton, Big Bear Lake, CA*

PREP: 10 min. + chilling • **MAKES:** 2 servings

- 1 snack-sized cup (4 oz.) pineapple tidbits (or ½ cup cubed fresh pineapple)
- ⅓ cup chopped apple
- ⅓ cup cubed cantaloupe
- 10 green grapes, halved
- 6 fresh strawberries, quartered
- 1 medium kiwifruit, peeled and sliced

DRESSING

- 2 Tbsp. mayonnaise
- 2 Tbsp. sour cream
- 1½ tsp. sugar
- 1 tsp. orange juice
- ¼ tsp. lemon juice
- ¼ tsp. grated lemon or orange zest

Drain pineapple, reserving 1 tsp. juice. In a salad bowl, combine pineapple, apple, cantaloupe, grapes, strawberries and kiwi. In a small bowl, combine the dressing ingredients; add reserved pineapple juice and mix well. Refrigerate fruit and dressing until chilled. Just before serving, pour the dressing over fruit and toss to coat.

1 CUP 136 cal., 2g fat (1g sat. fat), 7mg chol., 140mg sod., 28g carb. (22g sugars, 4g fiber), 3g pro.

TOMATO AVOCADO SALAD

CRUNCHY ASIAN COLESLAW

Go beyond traditional creamy coleslaw and try a flavorful twist. It's the perfect addition to an Asian-themed meal.
—Erin Chilcoat, Central Islip, NY

PREP: 15 min. + chilling • **MAKES:** 2 servings

- 1 cup shredded Chinese or napa cabbage
- ½ cup sliced water chestnuts, chopped
- ½ small zucchini, julienned
- 2 Tbsp. chopped green pepper
- 4½ tsp. rice vinegar
- 1 tsp. sugar
- 1 tsp. sesame seeds, toasted
- 1 tsp. reduced-sodium soy sauce
- ½ tsp. sesame oil
  Dash crushed red pepper flakes

In a small bowl, combine cabbage, water chestnuts, zucchini and green pepper. In another small bowl, whisk the remaining ingredients. Drizzle over salad; toss to coat. Refrigerate for at least 1 hour.
1 CUP 65 cal., 2g fat (0 sat. fat), 0 chol., 120mg sod., 11g carb. (5g sugars, 2g fiber), 2g pro.
DIABETIC EXCHANGES 2 vegetable.

BLT SALAD

Anyone who loves a BLT is sure to enjoy this! I keep the prepared ingredients in separate containers in the fridge, then just toss together one or more servings whenever needed.
—Mary Sigfusson, Mankato, MN

PREP: 25 min. + chilling • **MAKES:** 2 servings

- ⅔ cup uncooked spiral pasta
- 5 bacon strips, chopped
- 1 small tomato, seeded and chopped
- 3 Tbsp. ranch salad dressing
- 1 cup torn romaine

1. Cook pasta according to the package directions. Meanwhile, in a large skillet, cook bacon over medium heat until crisp. Remove to paper towels with a slotted spoon to drain.
2. Drain pasta and rinse in cold water; place in a large bowl. Add the bacon, tomato and dressing. Toss to coat. Refrigerate until serving.
3. Just before serving, add romaine and toss to coat.
1⅓ CUPS 315 cal., 19g fat (4g sat. fat), 21mg chol., 552mg sod., 25g carb. (3g sugars, 2g fiber), 10g pro.

TOMATO AVOCADO SALAD

One day when avocados were on sale at the supermarket, I grabbed some and came up with a new recipe. It's a nice change from a typical lettuce salad, plus it's quick to make.
—Pamela Raybon, Edna, TX

PREP: 20 min. + chilling • **MAKES:** 2 servings

- 1½ tsp. lemon juice
- ¾ tsp. lime juice
- ⅛ to ¼ tsp. garlic powder
- ⅛ tsp. salt
- ⅛ tsp. pepper
- ½ cup cubed tomato
- ¼ cup chopped red onion
- 1 medium ripe avocado, peeled and cubed

In a bowl, combine lemon juice, lime juice, garlic powder, salt and pepper. Add the remaining ingredients; toss gently to coat. Refrigerate for 30 minutes before serving.
1 CUP 173 cal., 15g fat (2g sat. fat), 0 chol., 163mg sod., 11g carb. (3g sugars, 5g fiber), 3g pro.
DIABETIC EXCHANGES 3 fat, 1 vegetable.

ASIAN CUCUMBER SALAD

This colorful cucumber dish makes a simple, cool side when we have stir-fry for dinner.
—Tari Ambler, Shorewood, IL

PREP: 15 min. + chilling • **MAKES:** 2 servings

- 4½ tsp. rice vinegar
- ½ tsp. honey
- ¼ tsp. sesame oil
- ¼ tsp. reduced-sodium soy sauce
  Dash salt and pepper
- ½ large cucumber, julienned
- ½ medium sweet red pepper, julienned
  Black and white sesame seeds

In a serving bowl, combine the vinegar, honey, oil, soy sauce, salt and pepper. Add cucumber and red pepper; stir to coat. Cover and refrigerate for at least 30 minutes, stirring occasionally. Garnish with sesame seeds.
¾ CUP 34 cal., 1g fat (0 sat. fat), 0 chol., 101mg sod., 7g carb. (4g sugars, 1g fiber), 1g pro.
DIABETIC EXCHANGES 1 vegetable.

CRUNCHY ASIAN
COLESLAW

THAI-STYLE GREEN BEANS

Two for Thai, anyone? Peanut butter, soy sauce and hoisin sauce flavor this quick and fabulous bean dish.
—*Candace McMenamin, Lexington, SC*

....

TAKES: 20 min. • **MAKES:** 2 servings

- 1 Tbsp. reduced-sodium soy sauce
- 1 Tbsp. hoisin sauce
- 1 Tbsp. creamy peanut butter
- ⅛ tsp. crushed red pepper flakes
- 1 Tbsp. chopped shallot
- 1 tsp. minced fresh gingerroot
- 1 Tbsp. canola oil
- ½ lb. fresh green beans, trimmed
  Optional: Minced fresh cilantro and chopped dry roasted peanuts

1. In a small bowl, combine the soy sauce, hoisin sauce, peanut butter and red pepper flakes; set aside.

2. In a small skillet, saute shallot and ginger in oil over medium heat for 2 minutes or until crisp-tender. Add green beans; cook and stir for 3 minutes or until crisp-tender. Add sauce; toss to coat. Sprinkle with cilantro and peanuts if desired.

1 CUP 168 cal., 12g fat (1g sat. fat), 0 chol., 476mg sod., 14g carb. (3g sugars, 4g fiber), 5g pro.

"Salty, sweet, crispy, spicy...in the tradition of Thai cooking, this recipe has it all. Thanks so much. Will definitely make it again!"

JAGIWAR, TASTEOFHOME.COM

SIDE DISHES
FOR TWO

Rounding out your meal with a small but
scrumptious side is easier than you may
think. Rely on these doubly delightful
veggies, pasta dishes and more!

CHEDDAR BASIL
CAULIFLOWER

CHEDDAR BASIL CAULIFLOWER

If you grow your own basil or like to keep it on hand, you'll want to save some for a side of flavorful, versatile cauliflower. I love how this dish not only warms you up in winter but also is delicious in summer made with garden-fresh produce.
—David Harper, Clackamas, OR

TAKES: 20 min. • **MAKES:** 2 servings

2½ cups small fresh cauliflowerets
1 Tbsp. white wine or water
1½ tsp. minced fresh basil or
   ½ tsp. dried basil
1 tsp. water
1 tsp. canola oil
½ tsp. sugar
¼ tsp. salt
⅓ cup shredded cheddar cheese

In a small saucepan, combine the first 7 ingredients. Cover and cook over medium heat for 10-12 minutes or until cauliflower is tender, stirring once. Transfer to a small serving bowl; sprinkle with cheese.
¾ CUP 128 cal., 8g fat (4g sat. fat), 20mg chol., 446mg sod., 8g carb. (4g sugars, 3g fiber), 6g pro.
DIABETIC EXCHANGES 1 vegetable, 1 fat, ½ fat-free milk.

PARMESAN HERBED NOODLES

Looking for pasta that's quick to prepare, tastes great and goes well with all kinds of meats? Here's a recipe that does it all! Feel free to toss in additional ingredients, too. For example, sometimes I stir in slightly cooked red and green pepper strips and a quarter cup of peas.
—Denise Elder, Hanover, ON

TAKES: 20 min. • **MAKES:** 2 servings

1½ cups uncooked wide egg noodles
2 Tbsp. shredded Parmesan cheese
1 Tbsp. butter
1 Tbsp. olive oil
2 tsp. minced fresh basil or
   ½ tsp. dried basil
½ tsp. minced fresh thyme or
   ⅛ tsp. dried thyme
1 garlic clove, minced
¼ tsp. salt

In a small saucepan, cook egg noodles according to package directions; drain. Add remaining ingredients and toss to coat.
1 CUP 243 cal., 15g fat (6g sat. fat), 46mg chol., 444mg sod., 21g carb. (1g sugars, 1g fiber), 6g pro.

TENDER BISCUITS

TENDER BISCUITS

These golden delights for two are low in fat but full of all the tender goodness you expect from a homemade biscuit.
—Ane Burke, Bella Vista, AR

TAKES: 30 min. • **MAKES:** 2 biscuits

⅓ cup self-rising flour
1 Tbsp. grated Parmesan cheese
⅛ tsp. garlic salt
3 Tbsp. reduced-fat cream cheese
3 Tbsp. fat-free milk
1 Tbsp. fat-free plain yogurt

1. In a small bowl, combine the flour, Parmesan cheese and garlic salt. Cut in cream cheese until the mixture resembles coarse crumbs. Stir in milk and yogurt just until moistened.

2. Drop by scant ⅓ cupfuls 2 in. apart onto a baking sheet coated with cooking spray. Bake at 400° for 12-15 minutes or until golden brown. Serve warm.
1 BISCUIT 142 cal., 5g fat (4g sat. fat), 18mg chol., 497mg sod., 17g carb. (2g sugars, 0 fiber), 6g pro.
DIABETIC EXCHANGES 1 starch, 1 fat.

SPINACH RICE

I like to make this Greek-style rice when we're having steaks with mushrooms. It rounds out an elegant meal and can easily be doubled for guests.
—Jeanette Cakouros, Brunswick, ME

TAKES: 20 min. • **MAKES:** 2 servings

- 2 Tbsp. olive oil
- ½ cup chopped onion
- ¾ cup water
- 1 Tbsp. dried parsley flakes
- ¼ to ½ tsp. salt
- ⅛ tsp. pepper
- ½ cup uncooked instant rice
- 2 cups fresh baby spinach

1. In a saucepan, heat oil over medium-high heat; saute onion until tender. Stir in water, parsley, salt and pepper; bring to a boil. Stir in rice; top with spinach.

2. Cover; remove from heat. Let stand until rice is tender, 7-10 minutes. Stir to combine.

¾ CUP 235 cal., 14g fat (2g sat. fat), 0 chol., 326mg sod., 25g carb. (2g sugars, 2g fiber), 3g pro. **DIABETIC EXCHANGES** 3 fat, 1½ starch, 1 vegetable.

TEST KITCHEN TIP

For a bit of crunch, toss in a handful of chopped pecans or sliced almonds.

SWEET POTATO FRIES WITH BLUE CHEESE

As a kid I hated sweet potatoes—mostly because they came out of a can. When I learned of their health benefits, I began trying fresh ones with my husband. Now we enjoy fries topped with cinnamon sugar or cayenne pepper. We've also discovered how awesome they are with blue cheese!
—Katrina Krumm, Apple Valley, MN

TAKES: 25 min. • **MAKES:** 2 servings

- 1 Tbsp. olive oil
- 2 medium sweet potatoes (about 1¼ lbs.), peeled and cut into ½-in.-thick strips
- 1 Tbsp. apricot preserves
- ¼ tsp. salt
- 3 Tbsp. crumbled blue cheese

In a large skillet, heat oil over medium heat. Add the sweet potatoes; cook until tender and lightly browned, turning occasionally, 12-15 minutes. Add preserves, stirring to coat; sprinkle with salt. Top with cheese.

1 SERVING 246 cal., 11g fat (3g sat. fat), 9mg chol., 487mg sod., 34g carb. (15g sugars, 3g fiber), 5g pro.

SPINACH RICE

ROASTED POTATOES

ROASTED POTATOES

Whatever meat you're serving, these golden potatoes are bound to complement it. The lemon juice and thyme add fabulous flavor.
—*Sally Sue Campbell, Greenville, TN*

PREP: 10 min. • **BAKE:** 40 min.
MAKES: 2 servings

- 2 Tbsp. lemon juice
- 4 tsp. olive oil
- ½ tsp. dried thyme
- ½ tsp. garlic salt
- ⅛ tsp. pepper
- 6 small red potatoes (about ¾ lb.), quartered

Preheat oven to 450°. In a medium bowl, combine lemon juice, oil, thyme, garlic salt and pepper. Add potatoes; toss to coat. Place in a greased 8-in. square baking dish. Bake, uncovered, until potatoes are tender, about 40 minutes, stirring occasionally.

1 SERVING 173 cal., 9g fat (0 sat. fat), 0 chol., 335mg sod., 22g carb. (0 sugars, 0 fiber), 2g pro.
DIABETIC EXCHANGES 2 fat, 1 starch.

SAVORY ONION MUFFINS

I've baked my onion muffins more times than I can count. Everyone loves them!
—*Norma Saunders, Los Angeles, CA*

PREP: 20 min. • **BAKE:** 20 min.
MAKES: 2 muffins

- ⅓ cup chopped onion
- 1½ tsp. butter
- ½ cup biscuit/baking mix
- 1½ tsp. poppy seeds
- 3 Tbsp. 2% milk
- 2 Tbsp. beaten large egg, divided
- 3 Tbsp. sour cream
  Dash pepper
  Dash paprika

1. In a small skillet, saute onion in butter until tender; set aside. In a small bowl, combine the biscuit mix and poppy seeds. In another bowl, combine the milk and 1 Tbsp. egg. Stir into the dry ingredients just until moistened.

2. Coat muffin cups with cooking spray; fill three-fourths full with batter. Combine the sour cream, pepper and remaining 1 Tbsp. egg. Spoon onion over muffin batter; spread with sour cream mixture. Sprinkle with paprika.

3. Bake at 400° for 18-20 minutes or until a toothpick comes out clean. Cool for 5 minutes before removing from pan to a wire rack. Serve warm.

1 SERVING 220 cal., 11g fat (4g sat. fat), 77mg chol., 451mg sod., 25g carb. (5g sugars, 1g fiber), 7g pro.

MACARONI & CHEESE

This is one of the dishes that our family calls a Mama recipe. My mother rarely consulted a cookbook, and when asked for a recipe, she could only estimate. I've reduced the ingredients in her cheesy macaroni so it serves two, but it can easily be doubled.
—*Betty Allen, East Point, GA*

PREP: 10 min. • **BAKE:** 30 min.
MAKES: 2 servings

- 1½ cups cooked elbow macaroni
- 1 cup shredded sharp cheddar cheese
- ½ cup whole milk
- 1 large egg, lightly beaten
- ½ tsp. salt
- 1 Tbsp. butter

Preheat oven to 350°. In a medium bowl, combine macaroni, cheddar cheese, milk, egg and salt; mix well. Pour into a greased 1-qt. shallow baking dish; dot with butter. Bake, uncovered, until a knife inserted in the center comes out clean, 30-35 minutes.
1½ CUPS 447 cal., 27g fat (18g sat. fat), 190mg chol., 1050mg sod., 30g carb. (4g sugars, 1g fiber), 21g pro.

SWEET ONION RICE CASSEROLE

Craving something warm and comforting? Indulge in a side of creamy onion and rice casserole. It's perfect for a cool evening.
—*Julie Rea, Battle Ground, WA*

PREP: 15 min. • **BAKE:** 45 min.
MAKES: 2 servings

- ⅓ cup uncooked instant rice
- 2½ cups chopped sweet onions
- 1 Tbsp. butter
- ¼ cup shredded Swiss cheese
- ¼ cup half-and-half cream

1. Cook rice according to the package directions. Meanwhile, in a large skillet, saute sweet onions in butter until tender. Stir in the cheese, cream and rice.
2. Transfer mixture to a 2-cup baking dish coated with cooking spray. Bake, uncovered, at 325° for 45-55 minutes or until golden brown.
1 CUP 277 cal., 13g fat (8g sat. fat), 43mg chol., 115mg sod., 32g carb. (14g sugars, 4g fiber), 8g pro.

SHIITAKE & BUTTERNUT RISOTTO

I think of this as a labor of love! The risotto needs a bit of extra attention, but as soon as you take your first bite, you'll know it was worth the effort.
—*Stephanie Campbell, Elk Grove, CA*

PREP: 25 min. • **COOK:** 25 min.
MAKES: 2 servings

- 1 cup cubed peeled butternut squash
- 2 tsp. olive oil, divided
  Dash salt
- 1¼ cups reduced-sodium chicken broth
- ⅔ cup sliced fresh shiitake mushrooms
- 2 Tbsp. chopped onion
- 1 small garlic clove, minced
- ⅓ cup uncooked arborio rice
  Dash pepper
- ¼ cup white wine or ¼ cup additional reduced-sodium chicken broth
- ¼ cup grated Parmesan cheese
- 1 tsp. minced fresh sage

1. Place squash in a greased 9-in. square baking pan. Add 1 tsp. oil and salt; toss to coat.
2. Bake, uncovered, at 350° until tender, 25-30 minutes, stirring occasionally.
3. Meanwhile, in a small saucepan, heat broth and keep warm. In a small skillet, saute mushrooms, onion and garlic in remaining 1 tsp. oil 3-4 minutes or until tender. Add rice and pepper; cook and stir for 2-3 minutes. Reduce heat; stir in wine. Cook and stir until all liquid is absorbed.
4. Add the heated broth, ¼ cup at a time, stirring constantly. Allow liquid to absorb between additions. Cook just until risotto is creamy and rice is almost tender, about 20 minutes. Stir in Parmesan cheese until melted. Add the squash and sage. Serve immediately.
¾ CUP 282 cal., 9g fat (3g sat. fat), 12mg chol., 567mg sod., 40g carb. (3g sugars, 3g fiber), 10g pro.

TEST KITCHEN TIP

If you add the cheese too early, the heat can cause it to break when fat separates out of the sauce. This can lead to a greasy and granular dish.

WHITE BEANS & SPINACH

WHITE BEANS & SPINACH

Here's a variation of a recipe I received from my Italian mother. I've prepared spinach like this for years—especially because my children love it this way!
—*Lucia Johnson, Massena, NY*

TAKES: 10 min. • **MAKES:** 2 servings

- 2 Tbsp. water
- 2 garlic cloves, minced
- 8 cups fresh spinach (about 6 oz.)
- ⅛ tsp. salt
  Dash cayenne pepper
  Dash ground nutmeg
- ¾ cup canned cannellini beans, rinsed and drained

Place water, garlic and spinach in a large skillet. Cook, covered, over medium heat just until tender, 2-3 minutes, stirring occasionally. Stir in remaining ingredients; heat through.

½ CUP 116 cal., 1g fat (0 sat. fat), 0 chol., 561mg sod., 21g carb. (1g sugars, 7g fiber), 7g pro.
DIABETIC EXCHANGES 1½ starch.

SQUASH RIBBONS

SQUASH RIBBONS

Steamed and well seasoned, these pretty ribbons will dress up your dinner plate. The strips of yellow summer squash and zucchini are easy to cut using a vegetable peeler or cheese slicer.
—Taste of Home *Test Kitchen*

....

TAKES: 15 min. • **MAKES:** 2 servings

- 1   **small yellow summer squash**
- 1   **small zucchini**
- 1   **Tbsp. butter, melted**
- ¼   **tsp. onion powder**
- ¼   **tsp. dried rosemary, crushed**
- ⅛   **tsp. salt**
- ⅛   **tsp. dried thyme**
- ⅛   **tsp. pepper**

1. With a vegetable peeler or metal cheese slicer, cut very thin slices down the length of each squash, making long ribbons. Place in a steamer basket; place in a saucepan over 1 in. of boiling water. Cover and steam until tender, 2-3 minutes.

2. In a small bowl, combine the butter, onion powder, rosemary, salt, thyme and pepper. Add squash and toss to coat.
¾ CUP 80 cal., 6g fat (4g sat. fat), 15mg chol., 206mg sod., 5g carb. (4g sugars, 2g fiber), 2g pro.
DIABETIC EXCHANGES 1½ fat, 1 vegetable.

PEA POD CARROT MEDLEY

We grow pea pods, and I wanted to use them in something other than stir-fries. A simple veggie side dish was the answer. I've received many compliments on its citrusy glaze and fresh flavor.
—Josie Smith, Winamac, IN

....

TAKES: 25 min. • **MAKES:** 2 servings

- 2   **medium carrots, sliced**
- 2   **cups fresh sugar snap peas, trimmed**
- 1   **tsp. cornstarch**
- ⅓   **cup orange juice**
- 2   **tsp. reduced-sodium soy sauce**
- ¼   **tsp. salt**
- ½   **tsp. grated orange zest**

1. Place carrots and water to cover in a small saucepan; bring to a boil. Reduce heat; simmer, covered, 5 minutes. Add peas; simmer, covered, until peas are crisp-tender, 2-3 minutes. Drain and remove vegetables from pan; set aside.

2. In same pan, mix remaining ingredients until cornstarch is dissolved; bring to a boil. Cook and stir until thickened, 1-2 minutes. Add vegetables; toss to coat.
1 CUP 119 cal., 1g fat (0 sat. fat), 0 chol., 535mg sod., 23g carb. (12g sugars, 6g fiber), 6g pro.
DIABETIC EXCHANGES 2 vegetable, ½ fruit.

"This was great! I served the side dish with black-bean burgers, and it was terrific."
GUINEAFOWLMAMA, TASTEOFHOME.COM

TANGY BAKED BEANS

You won't want plain canned beans again after you jazz them up with bacon, coffee, brown sugar and more.
—*Dean Copeland, Ochlocknee, GA*

PREP: 10 min. • **BAKE:** 25 min.
MAKES: 2 servings

- 2 bacon strips, cut into 1-in. pieces
- 2 Tbsp. strong brewed coffee
- 4 tsp. brown sugar
- 1 tsp. cider vinegar
- ¼ tsp. ground mustard
- ⅛ tsp. salt
- 1 can (8.3 oz.) baked beans, undrained
- ½ cup chopped onion

1. In a small skillet, cook the bacon over medium heat until partially cooked but not crisp. Drain on paper towels. Meanwhile, in a small saucepan, combine the coffee, brown sugar, vinegar, mustard and salt. Bring to a boil; cook and stir for 2-3 minutes or until sugar is dissolved. Stir in baked beans and onion.

2. Divide the bean mixture between two 6-oz. ramekins or custard cups coated with cooking spray. Top with bacon. Bake at 350° for 25-30 minutes or until bubbly.

½ CUP 213 cal., 5g fat (2g sat. fat), 14mg chol., 741mg sod., 36g carb. (19g sugars, 7g fiber), 9g pro. **DIABETIC EXCHANGES** 2 starch, 1 vegetable, ½ lean meat.

CREAMY TWICE-BAKED POTATOES

With plenty of cream cheese and sour cream in the filling, these special potatoes taste as good as they look.
—*Linda Wheeler, Harrisburg, PA*

PREP: 1¼ hours • **BAKE:** 20 min.
MAKES: 2 servings

- 2 medium baking potatoes
- 2 Tbsp. butter, softened
- 1 Tbsp. 2% milk
- ¼ tsp. salt
- 3 oz. cream cheese, cubed
- 2 Tbsp. sour cream
  Paprika
  Optional: Minced fresh parsley and green onions

1. Preheat oven to 350°. Pierce potatoes and bake on a baking sheet until tender, about 1 hour. When cool enough to handle, cut a thin slice off the top of each potato and discard. Scoop out the pulp, leaving a thin shell.

2. In a small bowl, mash the pulp with butter, milk and salt. Stir in cream cheese and sour cream. Spoon into potato shells. Sprinkle with paprika.

3. Place the potatoes on a baking sheet. Bake, uncovered, until heated through and tops are golden brown, 20-25 minutes. If desired, sprinkle with minced parsley and green onions.

1 SERVING 452 cal., 29g fat (18g sat. fat), 88mg chol., 561mg sod., 40g carb. (5g sugars, 3g fiber), 8g pro.

TANGY BAKED BEANS

**MICROWAVED
POULTRY DRESSING**

SCENTED RICE IN BAKED PUMPKIN

Here's a real showpiece for autumn menus. It's a delicious way to celebrate the season.
—*Lynn Heisel, Jackson, MO*

PREP: 30 min. • **BAKE:** 35 min.
MAKES: 2 servings

- 1 small pie pumpkin (about 2 lbs.)
- 1 Tbsp. olive oil
- ½ cup uncooked brown rice
- 1 cup water
- ¼ cup coarsely chopped pecans, toasted
- 3 dried apricots, chopped
- 2 Tbsp. raisins
- ¼ tsp. salt
- ¼ tsp. curry powder
- ⅛ tsp. ground cinnamon
- ⅛ tsp. ground cardamom, optional
- ⅛ tsp. ground cumin

1. Wash pie pumpkin; cut into 6 wedges. Remove the loose fibers and seeds from the inside; discard seeds or save them for toasting. Brush wedges with oil. Place on an ungreased 15x10x1-in. baking sheet. Bake at 400° for 35-40 minutes or until tender.
2. Meanwhile, in a small saucepan, bring rice and water to a boil. Reduce heat; cover and simmer for 20-25 minutes or until liquid is absorbed and rice is tender. Stir in the pecans, apricots, raisins, salt, curry, cinnamon and, if desired, cardamom.
3. Set 4 pumpkin wedges aside for another use. Sprinkle cumin onto remaining wedges; top with rice mixture.

1 SERVING 389 cal., 15g fat (2g sat. fat), 0 chol., 309mg sod., 62g carb. (13g sugars, 5g fiber), 7g pro.

TEST KITCHEN TIP

Use the leftover roasted pie pumpkin any way you would use cooked winter squash. Puree it and use it in soup, mash it for a side dish, or cube it and stir it into stuffing or pilaf.

MICROWAVED POULTRY DRESSING

Homemade stuffing in 15 minutes? You bet! Just use your microwave oven and this easy recipe. It is lower in sodium than packaged mixes and has ingredients you can tailor to suit your own taste.
—*Evelyn Clark, Sauk City, WI*

TAKES: 15 min. • **MAKES:** 2 servings

- 1 large egg
- ½ cup 2% milk
- 2 Tbsp. chopped celery
- 1 Tbsp. chopped onion
- ½ tsp. poultry seasoning
- ¼ tsp. rubbed sage
- ⅛ tsp. salt
  Dash pepper
- 1¾ cups unseasoned stuffing cubes

1. In a microwave-safe dish, beat egg and milk. Stir in celery, onion and seasonings. Add stuffing cubes; mix well. Let stand for 5 minutes.
2. Cover dish and microwave on high for 1 minute; stir. Cook for 1 minute; stir. Cook 30 seconds longer or until heated through.
½ CUP 236 cal., 5g fat (2g sat. fat), 111mg chol., 578mg sod., 38g carb. (6g sugars, 3g fiber), 11g pro.

SCENTED RICE IN
BAKED PUMPKIN

POACHED EGG BUDDHA BOWLS

My husband and I like to celebrate the arrival of spring by enjoying this breakfast in our backyard. Sometimes I toss in fresh peas and other seasonal delights.
—*Amy McDonough, Carlton, OR*

PREP: 5 min. • **COOK:** 65 min.
MAKES: 2 servings

- ¾ cup wheat berries
- 3½ cups water, divided
- 2 Tbsp. olive oil
- 2 Tbsp. lemon juice
- 1 Tbsp. thinly sliced fresh mint leaves
- ¼ tsp. salt
- ⅛ tsp. freshly ground pepper
- ½ cup quartered cherry tomatoes
- ½ cup reduced-fat ricotta cheese
- 2 Tbsp. sliced Greek olives
- 2 large eggs
  Optional: Additional olive oil and pepper

1. Place wheat berries and 2½ cups water in a large saucepan; bring to a boil. Reduce the heat; simmer, covered, until tender, about 1 hour. Drain; transfer to a bowl. Cool slightly.

2. Stir in oil, lemon juice, mint, salt and pepper; divide between 2 bowls. Top with tomatoes, ricotta cheese and olives.

3. To poach egg, place ½ cup water in a small microwave-safe bowl or glass measuring cup. Break an egg into water. Microwave, covered, on high 1 minute. Microwave in 10-second intervals until white is set and yolk begins to thicken; let stand 1 minute.

4. Using a slotted spoon, transfer the egg to 1 of the bowls. Repeat. If desired, drizzle with additional oil and sprinkle with more pepper.

1 SERVING 526 cal., 24g fat (5g sat. fat), 201mg chol., 563mg sod., 58g carb. (5g sugars, 10g fiber), 21g pro.

TEST KITCHEN TIP

Wheat berries are whole kernels of wheat. They cook up to a chewy texture with a hint of buttery flavor. Look for wheat berries near other whole grains; they're usually in the baking aisle in small packages.

BREAKFAST
FOR TWO

Mornings are twice as nice when they start with any of these easy, delicious, sized-right dishes—from golden waffles to exceptional eggs. Rise and shine!

VEGETABLE
FRITTATA

VEGETABLE FRITTATA

A simple side of fresh fruit makes a perfect refreshing counterpart to this cheesy, flavorful egg bake packed with veggies. My husband and I enjoy it just as much for late-night suppers as we do for brunch. Try swapping in your favorite egg substitute if you're cutting the fat in your diet.
—*Pauline Howard, Lago Vista, TX*

PREP: 15 min. • **BAKE:** 20 min.
MAKES: 2 servings

- 4 large eggs, beaten
- 1 cup sliced fresh mushrooms
- ½ cup chopped fresh broccoli
- ¼ cup shredded sharp cheddar cheese
- 2 Tbsp. finely chopped onion
- 2 Tbsp. finely chopped green pepper
- 2 Tbsp. grated Parmesan cheese
- ⅛ tsp. salt
  Dash pepper

1. Preheat oven to 350°. In a large bowl, combine all ingredients. Pour into a greased shallow 2-cup baking dish.
2. Bake, uncovered, until a knife inserted in the center comes out clean, 20-25 minutes.
½ FRITTATA 143 cal., 5g fat (3g sat. fat), 14mg chol., 587mg sod., 7g carb. (4g sugars, 1g fiber), 19g pro.

"I added corn and carrots. It was a delicious, light meal. Thank you, Pauline, for sharing the recipe."
ORBS, TASTEOFHOME.COM

BROWNIE BATTER OATMEAL

BROWNIE BATTER OATMEAL

Even people who aren't big fans of oatmeal will want to try this! With chocolaty richness from baking cocoa, every spoonful tastes more like a dessert treat than a breakfast. I top off each bowlful with a garnish of fresh raspberries and sliced almonds.
—*Kristen Moyer, Bethlehem, PA*

TAKES: 30 min. • **MAKES:** 2 servings

- 1 cup pitted dates, chopped
- 1 cup 2% milk
- ½ cup ground almonds
- ⅓ cup old-fashioned oats
- 2 Tbsp. baking cocoa
- 1 tsp. butter
- 1 tsp. vanilla extract
  Optional: Fresh raspberries and sliced almonds

1. Place dates in a heatproof bowl; cover with boiling water. Let stand until softened, about 10 minutes. Drain, reserving ⅓ cup liquid. Place dates and reserved liquid in a food processor; process until smooth.
2. In a small saucepan, whisk milk, almonds, oats, cocoa and ¼ cup date puree until blended. (Save remaining puree for another use.) Bring to a boil over medium heat, stirring occasionally. Remove from heat; stir in butter and vanilla. If desired, garnish with raspberries and sliced almonds.
¾ CUP 338 cal., 18g fat (4g sat. fat), 15mg chol., 73mg sod., 37g carb. (19g sugars, 7g fiber), 12g pro.

MEDITERRANEAN OMELET

This fluffy omelet gives us reason to rush to the breakfast table. For extra flair, add a chopped fresh herb such as basil, oregano or tarragon.
—*Milynne Charlton, Scarborough, ON*

TAKES: 10 min. • **MAKES:** 2 servings

- 4 large eggs
- ¼ cup water
- ⅛ tsp. salt
  Dash pepper
- 1 Tbsp. butter
- ¼ cup crumbled feta or goat cheese
- ¼ cup chopped tomato
- 1 green onion, chopped

1. In a small bowl, whisk the eggs, water, salt and pepper until blended. In a large nonstick skillet, heat the butter over medium-high heat. Pour in egg mixture. Mixture should set immediately at edge. As eggs set, push cooked portions toward the center, letting uncooked eggs flow underneath.

2. When eggs are thickened and no liquid egg remains, add cheese, tomato and green onion to 1 side. Fold omelet in half and cut into 2 portions; slide onto plates.

½ **OMELET** 236 cal., 18g fat (8g sat. fat), 395mg chol., 472mg sod., 3g carb. (1g sugars, 1g fiber), 15g pro.

BLUEBERRY PANCAKE SMOOTHIE

Have your blueberry pancakes and drink them, too! A smoothie loaded with fruit, oatmeal, maple syrup and cinnamon is great in the morning or at any time of day. If your berries are fresh instead of frozen, freeze the banana ahead of time.
—*Kailey Thompson, Palm Bay, FL*

TAKES: 5 min. • **MAKES:** 2 servings

- 1 cup unsweetened almond milk
- 1 medium banana
- ½ cup frozen unsweetened blueberries
- ¼ cup instant plain oatmeal
- 1 tsp. maple syrup
- ½ tsp. ground cinnamon
  Dash sea salt

Place the first 6 ingredients in a blender; cover and process until smooth. Pour into 2 chilled glasses; sprinkle with sea salt. Serve immediately.

1 CUP 153 cal., 3g fat (0 sat. fat), 0 chol., 191mg sod., 31g carb. (13g sugars, 5g fiber), 3g pro.
DIABETIC EXCHANGES 2 starch.

MEDITERRANEAN OMELET

HAM & EGG POCKETS

Thanks to convenient refrigerated crescent
roll dough, savory pockets of ham, egg and
cheese are a snap to prepare.
—Taste of Home *Test Kitchen*

....

TAKES: 20 min. • **MAKES:** 2 servings

- 1   **large egg**
- 2   **tsp. 2% milk**
- 2   **tsp. butter**
- 1   **oz. thinly sliced deli ham, chopped**
- 2   **Tbsp. shredded cheddar cheese**
- 1   **tube (4 oz.) refrigerated
      crescent rolls**

1. Preheat oven to 375°. In a small bowl,
combine egg and milk. In a small skillet, heat
butter until hot. Add the egg mixture; cook
and stir over medium heat until eggs are
completely set. Remove from the heat.
Fold in ham and cheese.
2. On a greased baking sheet, separate
crescent dough into 2 rectangles. Seal
perforations; spoon half of the filling down
the center of each rectangle. Fold in ends
and sides; pinch to seal. Bake until golden
brown, 10-14 minutes.
1 POCKET 345 cal., 22g fat (8g sat. fat),
132mg chol., 756mg sod., 23g carb. (5g
sugars, 0 fiber), 12g pro.

UPSIDE-DOWN PEAR PANCAKE

The pear tree in my yard inspires me to bake
with its fragrant fruit. This pancake works
best with a firm pear, not fully ripe.
—*Helen Nelander, Boulder Creek, CA*

....

TAKES: 30 min. • **MAKES:** 2 servings

- ½   **cup all-purpose flour**
- ½   **tsp. baking powder**
- 1   **large egg, room temperature**
- ¼   **cup 2% milk**
- 1   **Tbsp. butter**
- 1   **tsp. sugar**
- 1   **medium pear, peeled and thinly
      sliced lengthwise
      Confectioners' sugar**

1. Preheat oven to 375°. In a large bowl,
whisk flour and baking powder. In a
separate bowl, whisk egg and milk until
blended. Add to dry ingredients, stirring
just until combined.
2. Meanwhile, in a small ovenproof skillet,
melt butter over medium-low heat. Sprinkle
with sugar. Add pear slices in a single layer;
cook 5 minutes. Spread prepared batter
over pears. Cover and cook until top is set,
about 5 minutes.
3. Transfer pan to oven; bake until edges
are lightly brown, 8-10 minutes. Invert onto
a serving plate. Sprinkle with confectioners'
sugar. Serve warm.
½ PANCAKE 274 cal., 9g fat (5g sat. fat),
111mg chol., 197mg sod., 41g carb. (12g
sugars, 4g fiber), 8g pro.
DIABETIC EXCHANGES 2 starch, 1½ fat,
1 medium-fat meat, ½ fruit.

MANMOSA

Here's a guy-friendly adaptation of the refreshing mimosa. You'll need just three ingredients—beer, Triple Sec and juice.
—*Mike Dietiker, Elburn, IL*

....

TAKES: 5 min. • **MAKES:** 2 servings

- 1   bottle (12 oz.) beer, chilled
- 1   cup orange juice
- 2   oz. Triple Sec

Divide beer between 2 tall glasses. Add ½ cup orange juice and 1 oz. Triple Sec to each glass.

1⅓ CUPS 229 cal., 0 fat (0 sat. fat), 0 chol., 7mg sod., 31g carb. (28g sugars, 0 fiber), 1g pro.

CRESCENT SAUSAGE ROLLS

With sausage and cheese tucked inside golden crescent dough, these fun-to-eat rolls are winners with kids and adults alike.
—*Cherie Durbin, Hickory, NC*

....

TAKES: 30 min. • **MAKES:** 2 servings

- ⅓   lb. bulk pork sausage, cooked and drained
- 1   tsp. garlic powder
- 1   tsp. minced fresh parsley
- ½   tsp. grated Parmesan cheese
- ¼   tsp. dried basil
- 1   large egg, lightly beaten, divided
- 1   tube (4 oz.) refrigerated crescent rolls
- ½   cup shredded cheddar cheese

1. In a small bowl, combine the sausage, garlic powder, parsley, Parmesan cheese, basil and 2 Tbsp. beaten egg. Unroll the crescent dough and separate into 2 rectangles. Place on an ungreased baking sheet; seal perforations.

2. Spoon ½ of the sausage mixture into the center of each rectangle. Sprinkle with cheddar cheese. Roll up from a long side; pinch seam to seal. Brush with remaining egg.

3. Bake at 350° for 15-20 minutes or until golden. Cut into slices; serve warm.

1 SERVING 538 cal., 35g fat (13g sat. fat), 180mg chol., 1204mg sod., 26g carb. (4g sugars, 0 fiber), 27g pro.

BACON-BROCCOLI QUICHE CUPS

At my house, warm-from-the-oven quiche cups are a holiday tradition. The bonus? I can assemble them ahead of time and pop them in the freezer until the morning I'm ready to bake. For a tasty variation, substitute asparagus for the broccoli and use Swiss instead of cheddar.
—*Irene Steinmeyer, Denver, CO*

....

PREP: 10 min. • **BAKE:** 25 min.
MAKES: 2 servings

- 4   bacon strips, chopped
- ¼   cup small fresh broccoli florets
- ¼   cup chopped onion
- 1   garlic clove, minced
- 3   large eggs
- 1   Tbsp. dried parsley flakes
- ⅛   tsp. seasoned salt
    Dash pepper
- ¼   cup shredded cheddar cheese
- 2   Tbsp. chopped tomato

1. Preheat oven to 400°. In a skillet, cook bacon over medium heat until crisp, stirring occasionally. Remove bacon with a slotted spoon; drain on paper towels. Pour off drippings, reserving 2 tsp. in pan.

2. Add broccoli and onion to drippings in pan; cook and stir 2-3 minutes or until tender. Add garlic; cook 1 minute longer.

3. In a small bowl, whisk eggs, parsley, seasoned salt and pepper until blended. Stir in cheese, tomato, bacon and the broccoli mixture.

4. Divide mixture evenly between 2 greased 10-oz. ramekins or custard cups. Bake until a knife inserted in the center comes out clean, 22-25 minutes.

FREEZE OPTION Securely cover and freeze the unbaked quiche cups. To use, remove from the freezer 30 minutes before baking (do not thaw). Preheat oven to 400°. Bake as directed, increasing time as necessary for a knife inserted in the center to come out clean. Cover loosely with foil if tops brown too quickly.

1 SERVING 302 cal., 23g fat (9g sat. fat), 314mg chol., 597mg sod., 5g carb. (2g sugars, 1g fiber), 19g pro.

BLUEBERRY OAT WAFFLES

I love special recipes that make enough for just the two of us, like this one for yummy homemade waffles. The batter is great to use for pancakes as well.

—*Ruth Andrewson, Leavenworth, WA*

TAKES: 25 min. • **MAKES:** 4 waffles

⅔ cup all-purpose flour
½ cup quick-cooking oats
1 Tbsp. brown sugar
1 tsp. baking powder
½ tsp. salt
1 large egg
⅔ cup 2% milk
¼ cup canola oil
½ tsp. lemon juice
¼ cup ground pecans
½ cup fresh or frozen blueberries
Optional: Additional blueberries, chopped pecans, maple syrup and butter

1. In a bowl, combine flour, oats, brown sugar, baking powder and salt. In another bowl, combine egg, milk, oil and lemon juice; stir into dry ingredients just until combined. Fold in ground pecans and blueberries. Let stand for 5 minutes.

2. Bake mixture in a preheated waffle iron according to manufacturer's directions until golden brown. If desired, top with additional blueberries and chopped pecans, and serve with maple syrup and butter.

2 WAFFLES 691 cal., 44g fat (5g sat. fat), 100mg chol., 907mg sod., 64g carb. (15g sugars, 5g fiber), 14g pro.

BLUEBERRY OAT WAFFLES

BREAKFAST
BANANA SPLITS

BREAKFAST BANANA SPLITS

These bright cups are pretty enough for a formal brunch, yet simple and nutritious, too. Feel free to substitute different fruits and cereals—the possibilities are endless!
—*Renee Lloyd, Pearl, MS*

TAKES: 10 min. • **MAKES:** 2 servings

- 1 medium banana
- ⅓ cup each fresh blueberries, halved seedless grapes, sliced peeled kiwifruit and halved fresh strawberries
- 1 cup vanilla yogurt
- ½ cup granola with fruit and nuts
- 2 maraschino cherries with stems

Cut banana crosswise in half. For each serving, split each banana half lengthwise and place in a serving dish; top with ½ of each remaining ingredient.

1 SERVING 337 cal., 6g fat (1g sat. fat), 6mg chol., 96mg sod., 66g carb. (42g sugars, 8g fiber), 12g pro.

GRILLED BISTRO BREAKFAST SANDWICHES

I used to make a classic breakfast sandwich when my kids were still at home. Now that it's just my husband and me, I've added smoked Gouda, pear slices and spinach.
—*Wendy Ball, Battle Creek, MI*

TAKES: 30 min. • **MAKES:** 2 sandwiches

- 2 tsp. butter, divided
- 4 large eggs, beaten
- 4 slices (¾ in. thick) hearty Italian bread
- ⅛ tsp. salt
- ⅛ tsp. pepper
- 4 oz. smoked Gouda or smoked cheddar cheese, cut in 4 slices
- 1 medium pear, thinly sliced
- 4 slices Canadian bacon, cooked
- ½ cup fresh baby spinach

1. Heat 1 tsp. butter in a small nonstick skillet over medium heat; add eggs and scramble until set. Divide eggs between 2 slices of bread; sprinkle each with salt and pepper. Layer bread with cheese slices, pear slices, Canadian bacon and spinach. Top with remaining bread.

2. If using a panini maker, spread remaining butter on both sides of both sandwiches. Grill according to manufacturer's directions until golden brown and grill marks show, 6-8 minutes.

3. If using an indoor grill, spread half of remaining butter on 1 side of both sandwiches. Place buttered side down on grill; press down with a heavy skillet or other weight. Grill over medium-high heat until golden brown and grill-marked, 3-5 minutes. Remove the weight; spread remaining butter on the other side of both sandwiches. Return to grill, buttered side down; replace weight. Grill until golden brown, another 3-5 minutes.

1 SANDWICH 629 cal., 33g fat (17g sat. fat), 461mg chol., 1510mg sod., 44g carb. (11g sugars, 4g fiber), 38g pro.

EGGS LORRAINE

Here's one of my favorite special-occasion recipes. Each serving looks elegant baked in its own dish, and every bite is loaded with Canadian bacon and cheese.
—Sandra Woolard, DeLand, FL

··

PREP: 15 min. • **BAKE:** 25 min.
MAKES: 2 servings

- 4 slices Canadian bacon
- 2 slices Swiss cheese
- 4 large eggs
- 2 Tbsp. sour cream
- ⅛ tsp. salt
- ⅛ tsp. pepper
  Minced chives, optional

1. Preheat oven to 350°. Coat 2 shallow oval 1½-cup baking dishes with cooking spray. Line with Canadian bacon; top with Swiss cheese. Carefully break 2 eggs into each dish.
2. In a small bowl, whisk the sour cream, salt and pepper until smooth; drop by teaspoonfuls onto eggs.
3. Bake, uncovered, until the eggs are set, 25-30 minutes. If desired, sprinkle with minced chives.

1 SERVING 286 cal., 17g fat (6g sat. fat), 462mg chol., 1018mg sod., 3g carb. (3g sugars, 0 fiber), 28g pro.

MICHELADA

Like your drinks with a south-of-the-border vibe? Try this kicked-up beer cocktail that's a blend of Mexican lager, lime juice and hot sauce. There are many variations, but this easy one is perfect for rookie mixologists.
—Ian Cliffe, Milwaukee, WI

··

TAKES: 5 min. • **MAKES:** 1 Michelada

- Coarse salt
- Lime wedges
- Ice cubes
- 6 dashes hot sauce, such as Valentina or Tabasco
- 3 dashes Maggi seasoning or soy sauce
- 1 to 3 dashes Worcestershire sauce
- ¼ to ⅓ cup lime juice
- 1 bottle (12 oz.) beer, such as Corona, Modelo or Tecate

Place coarse salt in a shallow dish; run lime wedge around the rims of 2 cocktail glasses. Dip rims of glasses into salt, shaking off excess. Fill each glass with ice. In a small pitcher, combine hot sauce, Maggi seasoning, Worcestershire sauce and lime juice. Add beer. Pour into glasses over ice. Garnish with lime wedges. Serve immediately.

1 DRINK 165 cal., 0 fat (0 sat. fat), 0 chol., 137mg sod., 17g carb. (12g sugars, 0 fiber), 1g pro.

EGGS LORRAINE

BANANA FRUIT COMPOTE

BANANA FRUIT COMPOTE

My mother used to serve this compote when I was a child. My four children always ate more fruit when I dressed it up this way.
—Maxine Otis, Hobson, MT

PREP: 20 min. + chilling • **MAKES:** 2 servings

- **1 cup apricot nectar, divided**
- **Dash to ⅛ tsp. ground cloves**
- **Dash to ⅛ tsp. ground cinnamon**
- **1 Tbsp. cornstarch**
- **2 Tbsp. lemon juice**
- **1 firm banana, cut into ½-in. slices**
- **4 fresh strawberries, sliced**
- **1 kiwifruit, halved and thinly sliced**

1. In a small saucepan, bring ¾ cup apricot nectar, cloves and cinnamon to a boil. Combine cornstarch and remaining ¼ cup apricot nectar until smooth; gradually whisk into the nectar mixture. Return to a boil; cook and stir until thickened and bubbly, 1-2 minutes. Remove from the heat; stir in lemon juice. Cool.
2. Stir in banana, strawberries and kiwi. Cover and refrigerate for at least 1 hour before serving.
1 CUP 174 cal., 1g fat (0 sat. fat), 0 chol., 7mg sod., 44g carb. (29g sugars, 4g fiber), 2g pro.

CHICKEN SAUSAGE PATTIES

To lighten up breakfast patties, I substitute ground chicken for the pork sausage.
—Mary Webb, Longwood, FL

TAKES: 25 min. • **MAKES:** 2 servings

- **2 Tbsp. chopped onion**
- **¾ tsp. plus 2 tsp. olive oil, divided**
- **½ cup grated peeled tart apple**
- **1 Tbsp. minced fresh sage or ¾ tsp. rubbed sage**
- **¼ tsp. salt**
- **⅛ tsp. pepper**
- **Dash ground cinnamon**
- **¼ lb. ground chicken or turkey**

1. In a nonstick skillet, saute onion in ¾ tsp. oil until crisp-tender. Add apple; cook until tender, about 5 minutes. Let stand until cool enough to handle. Stir in seasonings. Crumble chicken over apple mixture and mix well. Shape into four ½-in.-thick patties.
2. In a skillet, cook patties in remaining oil over medium heat or until juices run clear.
2 PATTIES 159 cal., 11g fat (2g sat. fat), 38mg chol., 329mg sod., 7g carb. (5g sugars, 1g fiber), 9g pro.

CHEESY EGG QUESADILLAS

Start your day off with a little spice! These egg quesadillas are so easy to make and delicious for dinner, too.
—Barbara Blommer, Woodland Park, CO

TAKES: 25 min. • **MAKES:** 2 servings

- **3 large eggs**
- **3 Tbsp. 2% milk**
- **⅛ tsp. pepper**
- **1 Tbsp. plus 2 tsp. butter, divided**
- **4 flour tortillas (8 in.)**
- **½ cup refried beans**
- **¼ cup salsa**
- **⅔ cup shredded cheddar cheese**
- **Optional: Sour cream and additional salsa**

1. Preheat oven to 425°. Whisk together first 3 ingredients. In a large nonstick skillet, heat 1 Tbsp. butter over medium heat. Add egg mixture; cook and stir until eggs are thickened and no liquid egg remains. Remove from heat.
2. Place 2 tortillas on a baking sheet. Spread with beans; top with eggs, salsa, cheese and remaining tortillas. Melt remaining butter; brush over tops.
3. Bake until golden brown and cheese is melted, 10-12 minutes. If desired, serve with sour cream and additional salsa.
1 QUESADILLA 738 cal., 38g fat (18g sat. fat), 344mg chol., 1248mg sod., 67g carb. (3g sugars, 5g fiber), 30g pro.

CHEESY EGG
QUESADILLAS

SPEEDY CREAM OF WILD RICE SOUP

Add homemade touches to a can of potato soup to get comfort food on the table quickly. The result is a thick and creamy treat textured with wild rice and flavored with smoky bacon.
—*Joanne Eickhoff, Pequot Lakes, MN*

TAKES: 20 min. • **MAKES:** 2 servings

- ½ cup water
- 4½ tsp. dried minced onion
- ⅔ cup condensed cream of potato soup, undiluted
- ½ cup shredded Swiss cheese
- ½ cup cooked wild rice
- ½ cup half-and-half cream
- 2   bacon strips, cooked and crumbled

In a small saucepan, bring the water and onion to a boil. Reduce heat. Stir in potato soup, cheese, rice and cream; heat through (do not boil). Garnish with bacon.

1 CUP 333 cal., 18g fat (11g sat. fat), 68mg chol., 835mg sod., 24g carb. (5g sugars, 2g fiber), 15g pro.

TEST KITCHEN TIP

Switch it up! Stir in cubes of cooked ham, a handful of last night's veggies, or a dash of dried rosemary, thyme or parsley.

LUNCH
FOR TWO

Your noontime meal just might become the most delicious dish of the day! Whether packing an on-the-go lunch or getting cozy at home, you'll love these easy ideas.

BEST EVER GRILLED
CHEESE SANDWICHES

BEST EVER GRILLED CHEESE SANDWICHES

See if you don't think these are the best ever! Like to get creative? Experiment with different options for fillings, such as chives, a sprinkling of Parmesan cheese or Italian seasoning, or a spoonful of salsa.
—Edie DeSpain, Logan, UT

....

TAKES: 20 min. • **MAKES:** 2 servings

- 2 Tbsp. mayonnaise
- 1 tsp. Dijon mustard
- 4 slices sourdough bread
- 2 slices Swiss cheese
- 2 slices cheddar cheese
- 2 slices sweet onion
- 1 medium tomato, sliced
- 6 cooked bacon strips
- 2 Tbsp. butter, softened

1. Combine mayonnaise and mustard; spread over 2 bread slices. Layer with cheeses, onion, tomato and bacon; top with remaining bread. Spread the outsides of sandwiches with butter.
2. In a small skillet over medium heat, toast sandwiches until cheese is melted, 2-3 minutes on each side.
1 SANDWICH 714 cal., 48g fat (23g sat. fat), 111mg chol., 1291mg sod., 41g carb. (4g sugars, 3g fiber), 29g pro.

FLAVORFUL TOMATO SOUP

A tomato soup I discovered in a cookbook called for ingredients I didn't have on hand, so I improvised and came up with my own. I've since made—and shared—the recipe time and time again.
—Jean Sullivan, Denver, CO

....

TAKES: 15 min. • **MAKES:** 2 servings

- ¼ cup finely chopped onion
- 1 Tbsp. butter
- ¼ tsp. dried basil
- ¼ tsp. paprika
- ⅛ tsp. garlic powder
- 1 can (10¾ oz.) condensed tomato soup, undiluted
- 1 cup 2% milk
  Fresh basil leaves, optional

In a saucepan, saute onion in butter until tender. Add dried basil, paprika and garlic powder. Stir in soup and milk until well blended. Cook over medium heat until heated through, 6-8 minutes. If desired, top with fresh basil leaves.
1 SERVING 233 cal., 8g fat (5g sat. fat), 24mg chol., 989mg sod., 33g carb. (22g sugars, 2g fiber), 7g pro.

DIY RAMEN SOUP

DIY RAMEN SOUP

This favorite, prepared and served in a canning jar, is a healthier alternative to most commercial varieties. Feel free to customize the veggies.
—Michelle Clair, Seattle, WA

....

TAKES: 25 min. • **MAKES:** 2 servings

- 1 pkg. (3 oz.) ramen noodles
- 1 Tbsp. reduced-sodium chicken base
- 1 to 2 tsp. Sriracha chili sauce
- 1 tsp. minced fresh gingerroot
- ½ cup shredded carrots
- ½ cup shredded cabbage
- 2 radishes, halved and sliced
- ½ cup sliced fresh shiitake mushrooms
- 1 cup shredded cooked chicken breast
- ¼ cup fresh cilantro leaves
- 2 lime wedges
- 1 hard-boiled large egg, halved
- 4 cups boiling water

1. Cook ramen according to the package directions; cool.
2. In each of two 1-qt. wide-mouth canning jars, layer half of each ingredient in the following order: ramen noodles, chicken base, chili sauce, ginger, carrots, cabbage, radishes, mushrooms, chicken and cilantro. Place lime wedges and egg halves in 4-oz. glass jars or other airtight containers. Cover all 4 containers and refrigerate until serving.
3. To serve, pour 2 cups boiling water into each 1-qt. glass jar; let stand until warmed through or until chicken base has dissolved. Stir to combine seasonings. Squeeze lime juice over soup; place egg halves on top.
1 SERVING 401 cal., 14g fat (6g sat. fat), 153mg chol., 1092mg sod., 35g carb. (4g sugars, 2g fiber), 31g pro.

ITALIAN SAUSAGE ORZO SOUP

I'm always on the lookout for recipes that are full of taste and nutrition but short on prep time. This thick, chunky sausage soup is a winner with my whole family.
—*Deborah Redfield, Buena Park, CA*

....

PREP: 10 min. • **COOK:** 25 min.
MAKES: 2 servings

- ¼ lb. bulk Italian sausage
- ½ cup sliced fresh mushrooms
- ½ cup sliced zucchini
- ¼ cup chopped onion
- 1 tsp. olive oil
- 1 garlic clove, minced
- 1¼ cups reduced-sodium chicken broth
- 1 cup canned diced tomatoes, undrained
- ½ tsp. dried basil
- ⅛ tsp. pepper
- 3 Tbsp. uncooked orzo or small shell pasta
- 1 Tbsp. minced fresh parsley

In a large saucepan, cook the sausage, mushrooms, zucchini and onion in oil over medium heat until meat is no longer pink; drain. Add garlic; cook 1 minute longer. Add the broth, tomatoes, basil and pepper. Bring to a boil. Stir in pasta. Reduce heat; cover and simmer until pasta is tender, 15-20 minutes. Sprinkle with parsley.
1½ CUPS 236 cal., 10g fat (3g sat. fat), 23mg chol., 819mg sod., 25g carb. (8g sugars, 4g fiber), 12g pro.

COOL COUSCOUS SALAD

Here's a refreshing lunch or dinner for hot summer days or any time you want to eat light. I combine hearty couscous and tangy feta cheese for Mediterranean flair, and then I top it all off with my favorite balsamic vinaigrette for a punch of flavor.
—*Tiffany Blepp, Olathe, KS*

....

PREP: 15 min. + chilling • **MAKES:** 2 servings

- ⅓ cup water
- ¼ cup uncooked couscous
- ⅓ cup garbanzo beans or chickpeas, rinsed and drained
- ¼ cup seeded chopped cucumber
- 1 small plum tomato, seeded and chopped
- ¼ cup prepared balsamic vinaigrette
- 2 lettuce leaves
- 2 Tbsp. crumbled feta cheese

1. In a small saucepan, bring water to a boil. Stir in couscous. Cover and remove from the heat; let stand for 5-10 minutes or until water is absorbed. Fluff with a fork; cover and refrigerate for at least 1 hour.
2. In a small bowl, combine the garbanzo beans, cucumber, tomato and couscous. Pour vinaigrette over couscous mixture; toss to coat. Place lettuce leaves on 2 individual serving plates. Top with couscous mixture; sprinkle with cheese.
¾ CUP 212 cal., 7g fat (1g sat. fat), 4mg chol., 484mg sod., 29g carb. (5g sugars, 3g fiber), 7g pro.
DIABETIC EXCHANGES 2 starch, 1½ fat.

ITALIAN SAUSAGE ORZO SOUP

COBB SALAD CLUB SANDWICH

RASPBERRY-LEMON SPRITZER

Go beyond lemonade with a pretty pink thirst quencher that's tangy and not too sweet. I finish each glass with a lemon slice.
—*Margie Williams, Mount Juliet, TN*

....

TAKES: 15 min. • **MAKES:** 2 servings

- ½ cup fresh or frozen raspberries, thawed
- ⅓ cup sugar
- 2½ cups club soda, chilled
- ¼ cup lemon juice
  Ice cubes
- 2 lemon slices

1. Place raspberries and sugar in a food processor; cover and process until pureed. Strain, reserving juice and discarding seeds.
2. In a small pitcher, combine the club soda, lemon juice and raspberry juice. Serve in tall glasses over ice. Garnish with lemon slices.
1½ CUPS 148 cal., 0 fat (0 sat. fat), 0 chol., 66mg sod., 39g carb. (36g sugars, 0 fiber), 0 pro.

COBB SALAD CLUB SANDWICH

Can't decide whether you want a salad or a sandwich? You'll never have to choose again. With generous ingredients piled club-style high, this is a mouthwatering mashup. We affectionately call it the alpha "Clobb" sandwich!
—*Carmell Childs, Clawson, UT*

....

TAKES: 25 min. • **MAKES:** 2 servings

- 3 Tbsp. butter, softened
- 3 slices rustic Italian bread
- 3 slices cheddar or provolone cheese
- 2 pieces leaf lettuce
- 3 slices tomato
- 7 thin slices deli smoked peppered turkey breast
- ½ medium ripe avocado, peeled and sliced
- 3 Tbsp. blue cheese spread
- 7 thin slices deli oven-roasted chicken
- 7 thin slices deli ham
- 5 crisp cooked bacon strips
- 1 hard-boiled large egg, sliced

1. Spread the butter over 1 side of each bread slice. Place 1 slice cheese on each unbuttered side of bread. Toast bread slices, butter side down, in a large skillet or electric griddle over medium-low heat until golden brown, 4-5 minutes.
2. Layer 1 toast with lettuce, tomato, turkey and avocado. Top with another toast and spread with blue cheese spread. Top with chicken, ham, bacon and egg. Top with remaining toast, cheese side down. Cut sandwich in half, secure with toothpicks and serve.
½ SANDWICH 878 cal., 58g fat (26g sat. fat), 285mg chol., 2774mg sod., 32g carb. (5g sugars, 4g fiber), 58g pro.

CAULIFLOWER BROCCOLI CHEESE SOUP

Even my husband, who's never been a big fan of broccoli, digs in to this creamy soup. It's a perfect way to enjoy the produce from our vegetable garden.
—*Betty Corliss, Stratton, CO*

....

TAKES: 30 min. • **MAKES:** 2 servings

- ¾ cup small cauliflowerets
- ¾ cup small broccoli florets
- ¼ cup chopped onion
- ¼ cup halved thinly sliced carrot
- 1 to 2 Tbsp. butter
- 1½ cups 2% milk, divided
- ½ tsp. chicken bouillon granules
- ¼ tsp. salt
  Dash pepper
- 2 Tbsp. all-purpose flour
- ⅓ cup cubed Velveeta

1. In a large saucepan, cook cauliflower, broccoli, onion and carrot in butter until the vegetables are crisp-tender, about 5 minutes. Stir in 1¼ cups milk, bouillon, salt and pepper. Bring to a boil. Reduce heat; simmer, uncovered, until vegetables are tender, about 5 minutes, stirring occasionally.
2. Combine flour and remaining milk until smooth; add to saucepan. Bring to a boil; cook and stir until thickened, 1-2 minutes. Reduce heat; add cheese and stir until melted. Serve immediately.
1 CUP 267 cal., 15g fat (9g sat. fat), 48mg chol., 909mg sod., 23g carb. (13g sugars, 2g fiber), 12g pro.

> "Very good and creamy! I topped it with shredded cheddar cheese. It would be good with cooked diced ham or mushrooms."
>
> GUNSLINGER, TASTEOFHOME.COM

FLAVORFUL SLOPPY JOES

Like sloppy joes but not all the leftovers? Now you can make just enough for two hearty sandwiches. The sauce level in the meat mixture is low, making it a little less messy to eat on a bun.
—*Nancy Collins, Clearfield, PA*

....

TAKES: 25 min. • **MAKES:** 2 servings

- ½ lb. lean ground beef (90% lean)
- 2 Tbsp. chopped onion
- 2 Tbsp. chopped green pepper
- ½ cup ketchup
- 1½ tsp. brown sugar
- 1½ tsp. prepared mustard
- 1½ tsp. Worcestershire sauce
- 2 hamburger buns, split

1. In a small skillet, cook the beef, onion and green pepper over medium heat until meat is no longer pink; drain.
2. Stir in ketchup, brown sugar, mustard and Worcestershire sauce. Bring to a boil. Reduce the heat; simmer, uncovered, for 5 minutes. Serve on buns.
1 SANDWICH 379 cal., 11g fat (4g sat. fat), 56mg chol., 1112mg sod., 44g carb. (14g sugars, 2g fiber), 27g pro.
DIABETIC EXCHANGES 3 lean meat, 2 starch, 2 vegetable.

WATERMELON COOLER

Summertime means cooling off with a slice of watermelon and a glass of lemonade. Here are two warm-weather favorites in one refreshing beverage.
—*Darlene Brenden, Salem, OR*

....

TAKES: 10 min. • **MAKES:** 2 servings

- 1 cup lemonade
- 1½ cups seedless watermelon, coarsely chopped
- ½ cup crushed ice

In a blender, combine all ingredients; cover and process until smooth. Pour into chilled glasses; serve immediately.
1 CUP 86 cal., 0 fat (0 sat. fat), 0 chol., 12mg sod., 24g carb. (22g sugars, 1g fiber), 0 pro.

GRILLED JERK SHRIMP
ORZO SALAD

🍎 GRILLED JERK SHRIMP ORZO SALAD

It doesn't matter what the temperature outside is—you'll feel as if you're in the Caribbean when you take a bite of this deliciously seasoned salad.
—*Eileen Budnyk, Palm Beach Gardens, FL*

PREP: 25 min. • **GRILL:** 10 min.
MAKES: 2 servings

- ⅓ cup uncooked whole wheat orzo pasta
- ½ lb. uncooked shrimp (31-40 per lb.), peeled and deveined
- 1 Tbsp. Caribbean jerk seasoning
- 1 medium ear sweet corn
- 1 tsp. olive oil
- 6 fresh asparagus spears, trimmed
- 1 small sweet red pepper, chopped

DRESSING
- 1 Tbsp. water
- 3 Tbsp. lime juice
- 1 Tbsp. olive oil
- ⅛ tsp. salt
- ⅛ tsp. pepper

1. Cook orzo according to the package directions. Drain and rinse with cold water; drain well. Meanwhile, toss shrimp with jerk seasoning; thread onto metal or soaked wooden skewers. Brush corn with oil.

2. On a covered grill over medium heat, cook corn until tender and lightly browned, 10-12 minutes, turning occasionally; cook asparagus until crisp-tender, 5-7 minutes, turning occasionally. Grill shrimp until they turn pink, 1-2 minutes per side.

3. Cut corn from cob; cut asparagus into 1-in. pieces. Remove shrimp from skewers. In a large bowl, combine the orzo, grilled vegetables, shrimp and red pepper. Whisk together the dressing ingredients; toss with the salad.

2 CUPS 340 cal., 12g fat (2g sat. fat), 138mg chol., 716mg sod., 35g carb. (6g sugars, 7g fiber), 25g pro. **DIABETIC EXCHANGES** 3 lean meat, 2 starch, 1 vegetable, 1 fat.

HONEY-DIJON
CHICKEN SALAD

🍎 HONEY-DIJON CHICKEN SALAD

This delightful main-dish salad has a simple
sauce/dressing that adds sweet-tangy flavor.
If you prefer, change up the mix by tossing
in different kinds of vegetables.
—Janelle Hensley, Harrisonburg, VA

....

PREP: 15 min. • **BAKE:** 20 min.
MAKES: 2 servings

- ½   lb. chicken tenderloins, cut into
  ½-in. pieces
- 2   Tbsp. honey, divided
- 2   Tbsp. Dijon mustard, divided
- 3   cups torn leaf lettuce
- 2   hard-boiled large eggs, chopped
- 2   Tbsp. each chopped green, sweet
  orange and yellow pepper
- 1   Tbsp. chopped onion
- 2   tsp. sesame seeds

1. Preheat oven to 350°. Place chicken
in a greased 1½-qt. baking dish. Combine
1 Tbsp. each of honey and mustard; pour
over chicken. Cover and bake until chicken
is no longer pink, 20-25 minutes.

2. In a large bowl, combine the lettuce,
eggs, peppers, onion and sesame seeds;
divide between 2 plates. Top with the
chicken. Combine remaining 1 Tbsp. each
honey and mustard; drizzle over chicken.
2½ CUPS 301 cal., 9g fat (2g sat. fat),
279mg chol., 498mg sod., 25g carb. (19g
sugars, 2g fiber), 35g pro.
DIABETIC EXCHANGES 4 lean meat,
2 vegetable, 1 starch.

CHEESE-STUFFED BURGERS

Here's a sandwich that does traditional
burgers one better—with a surprise pocket
of cheddar! My family goes crazy for the
melted cheese center.
—Janet Wood, Windham, NH

....

TAKES: 25 min. • **MAKES:** 2 servings

- 1   Tbsp. finely chopped onion
- 1   Tbsp. ketchup
- 1   tsp. prepared mustard
- ¼   tsp. salt
- ⅛   tsp. pepper
- ½   lb. lean ground beef (90% lean)
- ¼   cup finely shredded cheddar cheese

- 2   hamburger buns, split
  Optional: Lettuce leaves and
  tomato slices

1. In a small bowl, combine the first
5 ingredients. Crumble beef over the
mixture and mix well. Shape into 4 thin
patties. Sprinkle cheese over 2 patties;
top with the remaining patties and press
edges firmly to seal.

2. Grill burgers, covered, over medium
heat 5-6 minutes on each side or until
a thermometer reads 160°. Serve on buns,
with lettuce and tomato if desired.
1 BURGER 357 cal., 15g fat (7g sat. fat),
84mg chol., 787mg sod., 25g carb. (4g
sugars, 1g fiber), 28g pro.
DIABETIC EXCHANGES 3 lean meat,
1½ starch, 1½ fat.

GRILLED PEPPER JACK CHICKEN SANDWICHES

With zesty pepper jack, smoky bacon and grilled chicken, these sandwiches taste like specialties from a restaurant.
—*Linda Foreman, Locust Grove, OK*

TAKES: 25 min. • **MAKES:** 2 servings

- 2 boneless skinless chicken breast halves (4 oz. each)
- 1 tsp. poultry seasoning
- 2 slices (½ oz. each) pepper jack cheese
- 2 center-cut bacon strips, cooked and halved
- 2 hamburger buns, split
- 4 lettuce leaves
- 4 slices tomato
- 1 slice onion, separated into rings
  Dill pickle slices, optional

1. Sprinkle chicken with poultry seasoning. Place chicken on oiled grill rack. Grill, covered, or broil 4 in. from the heat until a thermometer reads 165°, 4-7 minutes on each side. Top with cheese and bacon; cover and cook until the cheese is melted, 1-2 minutes longer.

2. Serve on hamburger buns with lettuce, tomato, onion and, if desired, pickles.

1 SANDWICH 335 cal., 11g fat (4g sat. fat), 85mg chol., 456mg sod., 25g carb. (4g sugars, 2g fiber), 33g pro. **DIABETIC EXCHANGES** 4 lean meat, 1½ starch.

TRIPLE BERRY INFUSED WATER

Make the most of summer's sweet bounty by infusing your water with a gorgeous blend of strawberries, blackberries and raspberries—or mix and match your favorite berries to suit your taste. The recipe fills a pitcher sized right for small households.
—*Taste of Home Test Kitchen*

TOTAL TIME: 5 min. + chilling
MAKES: 8 servings

- ½ cup sliced fresh strawberries
- ½ cup fresh raspberries
- ½ cup fresh blackberries
- 2 qt. water

Combine all ingredients in a large glass carafe or pitcher. Cover and refrigerate 12-24 hours.

1 CUP Due to its nature, this recipe has zero significant nutritional values.

GRILLED PEPPER JACK CHICKEN SANDWICHES

BAKED POTATO SOUP

I found our favorite soup in an unexpected place—a children's cookbook! This creamy comfort food is not only delicious but also scaled down to make a small amount that's perfect for my husband and me.
—Linda Mumm, Davenport, IA

....

TAKES: 20 min. • **MAKES:** 2 servings

- 2 medium potatoes, baked and cooled
- 1 can (14½ oz.) chicken broth
- 2 Tbsp. sour cream
- ⅛ tsp. pepper
- ¼ cup shredded cheddar cheese
- 1 Tbsp. crumbled cooked bacon or bacon bits
- 1 green onion, sliced

Peel potatoes and cut into ½-in. cubes; place half in a blender. Add chicken broth; cover and process until smooth. Pour into a saucepan. Stir in sour cream, pepper and remaining potatoes. Cook over low heat until heated through (do not boil). Garnish with cheese, bacon and onion.
1 CUP 277 cal., 8g fat (5g sat. fat), 28mg chol., 1061mg sod., 41g carb. (5g sugars, 4g fiber), 11g pro.

PEPPERONI BITES

I'm single and I love finding recipes that are both inexpensive and fast to fix. These little pizza-flavored pockets call for on-hand ingredients and bake in just 10 minutes in the toaster oven.
—Yvonne Roche, Lebanon, MO

....

TAKES: 20 min. • **MAKES:** 2 servings

- 3 Tbsp. tomato sauce
- ¾ tsp. olive oil
- ¼ tsp. dried oregano
- ⅛ tsp. garlic powder
- ¼ tsp. onion powder
- 1 tube (6 oz.) refrigerated flaky buttermilk biscuits
- 10 slices pepperoni
- 2 Tbsp. grated Parmesan cheese

1. In a small bowl, combine the tomato sauce, oil and seasonings. Cut each biscuit in half. Place 1 pepperoni slice on each half; fold dough over pepperoni and pinch edges to seal. Dip in tomato mixture.
2. Place in a shallow baking pan coated with cooking spray. Sprinkle with Parmesan cheese. Bake in a toaster oven at 450° for 10-12 minutes or until golden brown.
5 BITES 277 cal., 6g fat (2g sat. fat), 17mg chol., 1123mg sod., 43g carb. (1g sugars, 0 fiber), 12g pro.

ZIPPY EGG SALAD

ZIPPY EGG SALAD

Egg salad is always a tasty change of pace from the usual deli meat or peanut butter sandwiches. I like a touch of mustard and lemon juice for extra zip.
—Annemarie Pietila, Farmington Hills, MI

....

TAKES: 10 min. • **MAKES:** 2 servings

- 3 Tbsp. mayonnaise
- 1½ tsp. prepared mustard
- ⅛ tsp. salt
- ⅛ tsp. pepper
- ⅛ tsp. lemon juice
- 3 hard-boiled large eggs, coarsely chopped
- 1 Tbsp. minced green onion
- 2 slices bread
   Diced tomato, optional

Mix the first 5 ingredients. Stir in eggs and green onion. Serve on bread. If desired, top with tomato.
1 OPEN-FACED SANDWICH 332 cal., 24g fat (5g sat. fat), 281mg chol., 530mg sod., 16g carb. (3g sugars, 1g fiber), 12g pro.

GRILLED CAPRESE QUESADILLAS

Here's a quick and easy summer lunch that makes great use of garden-grown tomatoes. Feel free to swap in mozzarella or feta for the goat cheese, or make your quesadillas heartier by adding grilled chicken.
—Amy Mongiovi, Lititz, PA

....

TAKES: 20 min. • **MAKES:** 2 servings

- 4 whole wheat tortillas (8 in.)
- 6 oz. fresh mozzarella cheese, sliced
- 2 medium tomatoes, sliced and patted dry
- ⅓ cup julienned fresh basil
- ¼ cup pitted Greek olives, chopped
   Freshly ground pepper to taste

1. Layer half of each tortilla with cheese and tomatoes; sprinkle with basil, olives and pepper to taste. Fold tortillas to close.
2. Grill, covered, over medium-high heat until lightly browned and cheese is melted, 2-3 minutes per side.
1 QUESADILLA 535 cal., 25g fat (13g sat. fat), 67mg chol., 665mg sod., 52g carb. (5g sugars, 8g fiber), 25g pro.

BAKED
POTATO SOUP

PENNE WITH VEGGIES & BLACK BEANS

Meatless fare has never been so satisfying! This hearty stovetop dish is loaded with penne pasta, veggies and seasonings.
—*Vickie Spoerle, Carmel, IN*

TAKES: 25 min. • **MAKES:** 2 servings

- ¾ cup uncooked penne pasta
- ⅓ cup sliced zucchini
- ⅓ cup sliced fresh carrot
- 4 medium fresh mushrooms, sliced
- ½ small green pepper, thinly sliced
- ½ small onion, thinly sliced
- 1 small garlic clove, minced
- ¼ tsp. each dried basil, oregano and thyme
- ¼ tsp. salt
- ⅛ tsp. pepper
- 2 tsp. olive oil, divided
- 1 cup canned black beans, rinsed and drained
- ¼ cup chopped seeded tomato
- 2 Tbsp. shredded Parmesan cheese
- 2 tsp. minced fresh parsley

1. Cook pasta according to the package directions. Meanwhile, in a large nonstick skillet, saute zucchini, carrot, mushrooms, green pepper, onion, garlic and seasonings in 1 tsp. olive oil until crisp-tender. Stir in the beans.

2. Drain pasta; add to vegetable mixture. Add tomato and remaining olive oil; toss gently. Sprinkle with Parmesan cheese and minced parsley.

1⅓ CUPS 300 cal., 7g fat (2g sat. fat), 4mg chol., 643mg sod., 47g carb. (6g sugars, 8g fiber), 14g pro.

DINNER
FOR TWO

For a duo, dining on the perfect dinner doesn't have to mean going to a restaurant. Set a table for two and savor any of the home-cooked specialties found here!

MERLOT
FILET MIGNON

MERLOT FILET MIGNON

Here's a simple recipe that always looks and tastes exceptional. The rich, creamy merlot sauce adds elegance to the steaks. Round out your menu with a green salad and rolls.
—*Jauneen Hosking, Waterford, WI*

....

TAKES: 20 min. • **MAKES:** 2 servings

2   beef tenderloin steaks (8 oz. each)
3   Tbsp. butter, divided
1   Tbsp. olive oil
1   cup merlot
2   Tbsp. heavy whipping cream
⅛   tsp. salt

1. In a small skillet, cook steaks in 1 Tbsp. butter and the olive oil over medium heat until the meat reaches desired doneness (for medium-rare, a thermometer should read 135°; medium, 140°; medium-well, 145°), 4-6 minutes on each side. Remove and keep warm.
2. In the same skillet, add wine, stirring to loosen browned bits from pan. Bring to a boil; cook until the liquid is reduced to ¼ cup. Add cream, salt and remaining butter; bring to a boil. Cook and stir until slightly thickened and butter is melted, 1-2 minutes. Serve with steaks.
1 STEAK WITH 2 TBSP. SAUCE 690 cal., 43g fat (20g sat. fat), 165mg chol., 279mg sod., 4g carb. (1g sugars, 0 fiber), 49g pro.

YELLOW SQUASH TURKEY SALAD

This quickly became my favorite fast dinner. With a wonderful blend of flavors, colors and textures, the impressive salad goes together in just 10 minutes for a light and lovely meal on a busy weeknight.
—*Mildred Sherrer, Fort Worth, TX*

....

TAKES: 10 min. • **MAKES:** 2 servings

4   cups spring mix salad greens
¼   lb. thinly sliced deli smoked turkey, cut into 1-in. strips
1   small yellow summer squash, halved lengthwise and sliced
1   small pear, chopped
½   cup dried cranberries
⅓   cup honey-roasted sliced almonds
¼   cup cubed cheddar cheese
⅓   cup red wine vinaigrette

In a large bowl, gently combine the first 7 ingredients. Drizzle with vinaigrette and toss to coat. Serve immediately.
2 CUPS 490 cal., 17g fat (3g sat. fat), 37mg chol., 1170mg sod., 61g carb. (48g sugars, 7g fiber), 22g pro.

BALSAMIC-SALMON SPINACH SALAD

BALSAMIC-SALMON SPINACH SALAD

This spinach salad is really healthy and super fast to toss together. It's an absolute cinch to make after a long workday.
—*Karen Schlyter, Calgary, AB*

....

TAKES: 20 min. • **MAKES:** 2 servings

1   salmon fillet (6 oz.)
2   Tbsp. balsamic vinaigrette, divided
3   cups fresh baby spinach
¼   cup cubed avocado
1   Tbsp. chopped walnuts, toasted
1   Tbsp. sunflower kernels, toasted
1   Tbsp. dried cranberries

1. Drizzle salmon with 1 Tbsp. vinaigrette. Place on a broiler pan coated with cooking spray. Broil 3-4 in. from the heat until fish flakes easily with a fork, 10-15 minutes. Cut salmon into 2 pieces.
2. Meanwhile, in a large bowl, toss spinach with remaining vinaigrette. Divide between 2 plates. Top with the salmon, avocado, walnuts, sunflower kernels and cranberries.
1 SALAD 265 cal., 18g fat (3g sat. fat), 43mg chol., 261mg sod., 10g carb. (4g sugars, 3g fiber), 18g pro.
DIABETIC EXCHANGES 2 medium-fat meat, 2 fat, 1 vegetable.

> "I used the same quantities but divided the salmon and salad between four dinner-salad plates. Guests thought it was fancy."
> GVU, TASTEOFHOME.COM

SHRIMP PASTA PRIMAVERA

I think it's true—the way to a man's heart is through his stomach! So when my special someone is over for dinner, I like to serve something equally wonderful. I think this deliciously seasoned shrimp pasta has tons of flavor.
—*Shari Neff, Takoma Park, MD*

TAKES: 15 min. • **MAKES:** 2 servings

- 4 oz. uncooked angel hair pasta
- 8 jumbo shrimp, peeled and deveined
- 6 fresh asparagus spears, trimmed and cut into 2-in. pieces
- ¼ cup olive oil
- 2 garlic cloves, minced
- ½ cup sliced fresh mushrooms
- ½ cup chicken broth
- 1 small plum tomato, peeled, seeded and diced
- ¼ tsp. salt
- ⅛ tsp. crushed red pepper flakes
- 1 Tbsp. each minced fresh basil, oregano, thyme and parsley
- ¼ cup grated Parmesan cheese

1. Cook pasta according to the package directions. Meanwhile, in a large skillet, saute shrimp and asparagus in oil until shrimp turn pink, 3-4 minutes. Add garlic; cook 1 minute longer. Add the mushrooms, broth, tomato, salt and red pepper flakes; simmer, uncovered, for 2 minutes.

2. Drain pasta. Add pasta and seasonings to skillet; toss to coat. Sprinkle with cheese.

1 SERVING 581 cal., 32g fat (6g sat. fat), 89mg chol., 783mg sod., 49g carb. (4g sugars, 3g fiber), 24g pro.

NUTTY CHICKEN FINGERS

Please both your adult palate and your inner kid with homemade chicken strips. A crunchy pecan coating makes them stand out and doesn't require a lot of ingredients. Keep things easy by using prepared sauces for dipping—or have fun creating your own!
—*Beba Cates, Pearland, TX*

TAKES: 30 min. • **MAKES:** 2 servings

- ½ cup finely chopped pecans
- ⅓ cup crushed cornflakes
- 1 Tbsp. dried parsley flakes
- ⅛ tsp. garlic powder
- ⅛ tsp. salt
- 2 Tbsp. 2% milk
- ¾ lb. boneless skinless chicken breasts, cut into 1-in. strips

1. Preheat oven to 400°. In a shallow bowl, combine the first 5 ingredients. Place milk in another shallow bowl. Dip chicken in milk, then roll in pecan mixture.

2. Place in a single layer in an ungreased 15x10x1-in. baking pan. Bake, uncovered, until juices run clear, 12-15 minutes.

5 OZ. COOKED CHICKEN 436 cal., 24g fat (3g sat. fat), 96mg chol., 346mg sod., 18g carb. (3g sugars, 3g fiber), 38g pro.

SHRIMP PASTA PRIMAVERA

**SPICE-RUBBED
LAMB CHOPS**

SPICE-RUBBED LAMB CHOPS

Lamb chops are one of my absolute favorite meals, and the spice rub in this recipe adds even more appeal. My two daughters love watching me prepare the meat and then sampling the results.
—*Nareman Dietz, Beverly Hills, MI*

....

PREP: 15 min. + chilling • **BAKE:** 5 min.
MAKES: 2 servings

- 2 tsp. lemon juice
- 2 tsp. Worcestershire sauce
- 1½ tsp. pepper
- 1¼ tsp. ground cumin
- 1¼ tsp. curry powder
- 1 garlic clove, minced
- ½ tsp. sea salt
- ½ tsp. onion powder
- ½ tsp. crushed red pepper flakes
- 4 lamb rib chops
- 1 Tbsp. olive oil

1. Mix first 9 ingredients; spread over lamb chops. Refrigerate, covered, overnight.

2. Preheat oven to 450°. In an ovenproof skillet, heat the olive oil over medium-high heat; brown lamb chops, about 2 minutes per side. Transfer to oven; roast until desired doneness (for medium-rare, a thermometer should read 135°; medium, 140°), 3-4 minutes.
2 LAMB CHOPS 290 cal., 17g fat (4g sat. fat), 90mg chol., 620mg sod., 5g carb. (1g sugars, 2g fiber), 29g pro.
DIABETIC EXCHANGES 4 lean meat, 1½ fat.

FLAVORFUL SALMON FILLETS

Here's a fabulous way to grill salmon. A simple marinade pumps up the taste while keeping the fillets moist and tender.
—*Krista Frank, Rhododendron, OR*

....

TAKES: 30 min. • **MAKES:** 2 servings

- ¼ cup packed brown sugar
- ¼ cup reduced-sodium soy sauce
- 3 Tbsp. unsweetened pineapple juice
- 3 Tbsp. red wine vinegar
- 1 Tbsp. lemon juice

- 3 garlic cloves, minced
- 1 tsp. ground ginger
- 1 tsp. pepper
- ¼ tsp. hot pepper sauce
- 2 salmon fillets (1 in. thick and 6 oz. each)

1. In a bowl or shallow dish, combine the first 9 ingredients. Add salmon and turn to coat. Cover and refrigerate for 15 minutes, turning once.
2. Drain salmon, discarding marinade. Place salmon on oiled grill rack, skin side down. Grill, covered, over medium heat or broil 4 in. from the heat until fish just begins to flake easily with a fork, 13-15 minutes.
1 FILLET 330 cal., 18g fat (4g sat. fat), 100mg chol., 204mg sod., 4g carb. (3g sugars, 0 fiber), 34g pro.
DIABETIC EXCHANGES 5 lean meat.

TASTY TURKEY & MUSHROOMS

Fresh mushrooms star in this tender turkey entree that comes together in 15 minutes. Served with a side of brown rice, it makes a light but satisfying dinner.
—*Nancy Zimmerman,*
Cape May Court House, NJ

TAKES: 15 min. • **MAKES:** 2 servings

- 1   garlic clove, minced
- 1   Tbsp. butter
- ½   lb. boneless skinless turkey breast, cut into 2-in. strips
- ¾   cup reduced-sodium beef broth
- 1   Tbsp. tomato paste
- 2   cups sliced fresh mushrooms
- ⅛   tsp. salt

In a large nonstick skillet, saute garlic in butter until tender. Add turkey; cook until juices run clear. Remove and keep warm. Add the broth, tomato paste, mushrooms and salt to skillet; cook for 3-5 minutes or until mushrooms are tender, stirring occasionally. Return turkey to the pan and heat through.

1 CUP 209 cal., 7g fat (4g sat. fat), 88mg chol., 435mg sod., 5g carb. (3g sugars, 1g fiber), 31g pro.
DIABETIC EXCHANGES 3 lean meat, 1½ fat, 1 vegetable.

FOUR-CHEESE STUFFED SHELLS

More cheese, please! You'll get your fill from saucy jumbo pasta shells loaded with four kinds—ricotta, Asiago, cottage cheese and mozzarella. Do the prep work, and then freeze according to the recipe directions to have a ready-to-bake meal.
—Taste of Home *Test Kitchen*

PREP: 20 min. • **BAKE:** 25 min.
MAKES: 2 servings

- 6   uncooked jumbo pasta shells
- ½   cup shredded part-skim mozzarella cheese, divided
- ¼   cup shredded Asiago cheese
- ¼   cup ricotta cheese
- ¼   cup 4% cottage cheese
- 1   Tbsp. minced chives
- 1   pkg. (10 oz.) frozen chopped spinach, thawed and squeezed dry
- 1   cup meatless spaghetti sauce

1. Preheat oven to 350°. Cook the pasta shells according to the package directions. Meanwhile, in a small bowl, combine ¼ cup mozzarella cheese, Asiago cheese, ricotta cheese, cottage cheese, chives and ½ cup spinach (save the remaining spinach for another use).
2. Spread ½ cup spaghetti sauce into a shallow 1½-qt. baking dish coated with cooking spray. Drain pasta; stuff with cheese mixture. Arrange in prepared dish. Top with remaining spaghetti sauce and mozzarella cheese.
3. Cover and bake until heated through, 25-30 minutes.

FREEZE OPTION Cool the unbaked pasta shells; cover and freeze. To use, partially thaw in the refrigerator overnight. Remove from refrigerator 30 minutes before baking. Preheat oven to 350°. Bake as directed, increasing the time as necessary to heat through and for a thermometer inserted in the center of 2 or 3 shells to read 165°.

3 STUFFED SHELLS 376 cal., 14g fat (9g sat. fat), 49mg chol., 959mg sod., 39g carb. (13g sugars, 4g fiber), 25g pro.

GREEK BROWN & WILD RICE BOWLS

GREEK BROWN & WILD RICE BOWLS

Enjoy the Mediterranean in a bowl! This easy dish is simple but packs in so much flavor. For a hand-held variation, leave out the rice medley and tuck the remaining ingredients into your favorite pita pocket.
—*Darla Andrews, Schertz, TX*

TAKES: 15 min. • **MAKES:** 2 servings

  1 pkg. (8½ oz.) ready-to-serve whole grain brown and wild rice medley
  ¼ cup Greek vinaigrette, divided
  ½ medium ripe avocado, peeled and sliced
  ¾ cup cherry tomatoes, halved
  ¼ cup crumbled feta cheese
  ¼ cup pitted Greek olives, sliced
      Minced fresh parsley, optional

In a microwave-safe bowl, combine the rice mix and 2 Tbsp. Greek vinaigrette. Cover and cook on high until heated through, about 2 minutes. Divide between 2 bowls. Top with avocado, tomatoes, cheese, olives, remaining dressing and, if desired, parsley.
1 SERVING 433 cal., 25g fat (4g sat. fat), 8mg chol., 1355mg sod., 44g carb. (3g sugars, 6g fiber), 8g pro.

TEST KITCHEN TIP

These otherwise healthy bowls are high in sodium because of the prepared rice, dressing, feta cheese and Greek olives. Save on sodium by cooking rice from scratch and using an oil and vinegar dressing.

CHICKEN STRAWBERRY SPINACH SALAD

This pretty spinach salad features strips of grilled chicken, fresh strawberries and toasted almonds. A drizzle of sweet poppy seed dressing is the perfect finishing touch.
—*Ginger Ellsworth, Caldwell, ID*

....

TAKES: 30 min. • **MAKES:** 2 servings

- ¾ **lb. boneless skinless chicken breasts, cut into strips**
- ¼ **cup reduced-sodium chicken broth**
- ¼ **cup poppy seed salad dressing, divided**
- 2 **cups fresh baby spinach**
- 1 **cup torn romaine**
- 1 **cup sliced fresh strawberries**
- ¼ **cup sliced almonds, toasted**

1. Place chicken on a double thickness of heavy-duty foil (about 18x15 in.). Combine broth and 1 Tbsp. poppy seed dressing; spoon over chicken. Fold the edges of foil around chicken mixture, leaving the center open. Grill, covered, over medium heat until chicken is no longer pink, 10-12 minutes.

2. In a large salad bowl, combine spinach, romaine and strawberries. Add the chicken and remaining poppy seed dressing; toss to coat. Sprinkle with almonds.

2 CUPS 438 cal., 22g fat (3g sat. fat), 104mg chol., 386mg sod., 18g carb. (11g sugars, 5g fiber), 39g pro.

THAI CHICKEN STIR-FRY

Instead of getting Thai food at a restaurant, why not make your own at home? Thanks to a convenient frozen vegetable blend and pantry staples, you can treat yourself to an amazing stir-fry in minutes.
—*Sally Bailey, Wooster, OH*

....

TAKES: 25 min. • **MAKES:** 2 servings

- ½ **lb. boneless skinless chicken breasts, cut into 1-in. strips**
- 2½ **tsp. olive oil**
- 2 **cups frozen stir-fry vegetable blend, thawed**
- 2 **Tbsp. unsweetened apple juice**
- 2 **Tbsp. soy sauce**
- 2 **Tbsp. creamy peanut butter**
- 1 **Tbsp. brown sugar**
- 1 **tsp. garlic powder**
- ⅛ **tsp. ground ginger**
- ⅛ **tsp. cayenne pepper**
  Hot cooked rice

In a large skillet or wok, stir-fry chicken in oil for 3-4 minutes or until no longer pink. Stir in vegetable blend; cook, uncovered, for 4-6 minutes or until vegetables are tender. Meanwhile, in a small bowl, combine the apple juice, soy sauce, peanut butter, brown sugar, garlic powder, ginger and cayenne. Stir into chicken mixture; serve with rice.

1 CUP 382 cal., 16g fat (3g sat. fat), 63mg chol., 1100mg sod., 27g carb. (11g sugars, 5g fiber), 32g pro.

CHICKEN STRAWBERRY SPINACH SALAD

COWBOY CASSEROLE

Here's a great home-style dinner, especially for chilly nights. The scaled-down recipe gives you the comfort of a casserole without all the leftovers.
—*Donna Donhauser, Remsen, NY*

PREP: 15 min. • **BAKE:** 20 min.
MAKES: 2 servings

- ½ lb. lean ground beef (90% lean)
- 1 can (8¾ oz.) whole kernel corn, drained
- ⅔ cup condensed cream of chicken soup, undiluted
- ½ cup shredded cheddar cheese, divided
- ⅓ cup 2% milk
- 2 Tbsp. sour cream
- ¾ tsp. onion powder
- ¼ tsp. pepper
- 2 cups frozen Tater Tots

1. Preheat oven to 375°. In a large skillet, cook the beef over medium heat until no longer pink. Stir in the corn, soup, ¼ cup cheese, milk, sour cream, onion powder and pepper.
2. Place 1 cup Tater Tots in a greased 3-cup baking dish. Layer with the beef mixture and remaining Tater Tots; sprinkle with remaining cheese. Bake, uncovered, until bubbly, 20-25 minutes.

1 SERVING 714 cal., 38g fat (15g sat. fat), 120mg chol., 1675mg sod., 56g carb. (9g sugars, 6g fiber), 37g pro.

TEST KITCHEN TIP

Make this comforting dish your own by swapping in your favorite cream soup, trying a different cheese or adding a dash of dried herbs.

SKILLET TACOS

Love Mexican food? You'll want to make this twist on tacos every chance you get!
—*Maria Gobel, Greenfield, WI*

TAKES: 30 min. • **MAKES:** 2 servings

- 1 Tbsp. olive oil
- ¼ lb. lean ground turkey
- 2 Tbsp. chopped onion
- 2 Tbsp. chopped green pepper
- 1 can (8 oz.) tomato sauce
- ½ cup uncooked elbow macaroni
- ½ cup water
- ¼ cup picante sauce
- 2 Tbsp. shredded reduced-fat cheddar cheese
- ¼ cup crushed baked tortilla chip scoops
- ¼ cup chopped avocado
  Optional: Iceberg lettuce wedges and sour cream

1. Heat olive oil in a large nonstick skillet over medium-high heat; add turkey, onion and green pepper. Cook until vegetables are tender and turkey is no longer pink.
2. Stir in tomato sauce, macaroni, water and picante sauce. Bring to a boil. Reduce heat; cover and simmer until macaroni is tender, 10-15 minutes.
3. Divide between 2 bowls; top with cheese, tortilla chips and avocado. Serve with lettuce and sour cream if desired.

1 CUP 337 cal., 17g fat (4g sat. fat), 44mg chol., 861mg sod., 30g carb. (4g sugars, 5g fiber), 19g pro.

COWBOY CASSEROLE

CHICKEN PAELLA

PARMESAN PORK TENDERLOIN

I am of Danish descent and love all things pork, both old recipes and new. Here's a dish I came up with myself.
—*John Hansen, Marstons Mills, MA*

PREP: 25 min. • **COOK:** 25 min.
MAKES: 2 servings

- 1   pork tenderloin (¾ lb.)
- 6   Tbsp. grated Parmesan cheese
- 1   small sweet onion, sliced and separated into rings
- 1½   cups sliced fresh mushrooms
- 1   garlic clove, minced
- 2   tsp. butter, divided
- 2   tsp. olive oil, divided
- ¼   cup reduced-sodium beef broth
- 2   Tbsp. port wine or additional beef broth
- ⅛   tsp. salt, optional
- ⅛   tsp. each dried basil, thyme and rosemary, crushed
      Dash pepper
- ½   tsp. cornstarch
- 3   Tbsp. water

1. Cut tenderloin into ½-in. slices; flatten to ⅛-in. thickness. Coat with Parmesan cheese; set aside.
2. In a large skillet, saute sweet onion, mushrooms and garlic in 1 tsp. butter and 1 tsp. oil until tender; remove and keep warm. In the same skillet, cook the pork in remaining 1 tsp. butter and 1 tsp. oil in batches over medium heat until juices run clear, about 2 minutes on each side. Remove and keep warm.
3. Add beef broth to the pan, scraping to loosen browned bits. Stir in port wine or additional broth; add seasonings. Bring to a boil. Reduce heat; simmer, uncovered, for 5 minutes. Combine cornstarch and water until smooth; stir into pan juices. Bring to a boil; cook and stir until thickened, about 2 minutes. Serve with the pork and the onion mixture.
1 SERVING 388 cal., 19g fat (8g sat. fat), 118mg chol., 472mg sod., 11g carb. (6g sugars, 2g fiber), 43g pro.

CHICKEN PAELLA

Turmeric lends its distinctive flavor and bright golden color to this Spanish-style entree. Haven't tried arborio rice? You're sure to enjoy its creamy texture.
—*Taste of Home Test Kitchen*

PREP: 10 min. • **COOK:** 45 min.
MAKES: 2 servings

- 2   boneless skinless chicken thighs (about ½ lb.), cut into 2-in. pieces
- ½   cup cubed fully cooked ham
- ⅓   cup chopped onion
- ⅓   cup julienned sweet red pepper
- 1   Tbsp. olive oil, divided
- ½   cup uncooked arborio rice
- ½   tsp. ground turmeric
- ½   tsp. ground cumin
- ½   tsp. minced garlic
- ⅛   tsp. salt
- 1   cup plus 2 Tbsp. chicken broth
- ¾   cup frozen peas, thawed

1. In a large skillet, saute the chicken, ham, onion and red pepper in 2 tsp. oil until chicken is browned on all sides. Remove with a slotted spoon.
2. In same skillet, saute rice in remaining oil until lightly browned. Stir in turmeric, cumin, garlic and salt. Return meat and vegetables to pan; toss lightly. Add broth; bring to a boil. Reduce heat to medium; cover and simmer until the rice is tender, 30-35 minutes. Stir in peas.
1½ CUPS 516 cal., 17g fat (4g sat. fat), 99mg chol., 1242mg sod., 52g carb. (5g sugars, 4g fiber), 36g pro.

PARMESAN
PORK TENDERLOIN

HOMEMADE FISH STICKS

I am a nutritionist and needed a healthy fish fix. Moist inside and crunchy outside, these are great with low-fat tartar sauce and a side of oven fries or roasted veggies.
—*Jennifer Rowland, Elizabethtown, KY*

TAKES: 25 min. • **MAKES:** 2 servings

- ½ cup dry bread crumbs
- ½ tsp. salt
- ½ tsp. paprika
- ½ tsp. lemon-pepper seasoning
- ½ cup all-purpose flour
- 1 large egg, beaten
- ¾ lb. cod fillets, cut into 1-in. strips
  Butter-flavored cooking spray

1. Preheat oven to 400°. In a shallow bowl, mix bread crumbs and seasonings. Place flour and egg in separate shallow bowls. Dip fish in flour to coat both sides; shake off excess. Dip in egg, then in crumb mixture, patting to help coating adhere.
2. Place on a baking sheet coated with cooking spray; spritz with butter-flavored cooking spray. Bake 10-12 minutes or until fish just begins to flake easily with a fork, turning once.
1 SERVING 278 cal., 4g fat (1g sat. fat), 129mg chol., 718mg sod., 25g carb. (2g sugars, 1g fiber), 33g pro.
DIABETIC EXCHANGES 4 lean meat, 1½ starch.

LAZY LASAGNA

Traditional lasagna can require too much time on a busy evening. One day when I had a taste for it, I created a simplified version. It satisfied my craving!
—*Carol Mead, Los Alamos, NM*

TAKES: 30 min. • **MAKES:** 2 servings

- 1 cup spaghetti sauce
- ¾ cup shredded part-skim mozzarella cheese
- ½ cup 4% cottage cheese
- 1½ cups cooked wide egg noodles
- 2 Tbsp. grated Parmesan cheese
  Chopped fresh parsley, optional

1. Warm spaghetti sauce; stir in mozzarella and cottage cheeses. Fold in noodles. Pour into 2 greased 2-cup baking dishes. Sprinkle with Parmesan cheese.
2. Bake, uncovered, at 375° until bubbly, about 20 minutes. If desired, top with chopped parsley.
1 LASAGNA 399 cal., 16g fat (8g sat. fat), 68mg chol., 1120mg sod., 37g carb. (12g sugars, 3g fiber), 25g pro.

ZESTY BAKED CATFISH

Common pantry seasonings combine for a catfish dinner that's anything but basic.
—*Karen Conklin, Supply, NC*

TAKES: 20 min. • **MAKES:** 2 servings

- 1 tsp. canola oil
- 1 tsp. lemon juice
- 2 catfish fillets (6 oz. each)
- 1½ tsp. paprika
- ½ tsp. dried tarragon
- ½ tsp. dried basil
- ½ tsp. pepper
- ⅛ tsp. cayenne pepper
- ¼ tsp. salt

1. Combine the oil and lemon juice; brush over both sides of fillets. Combine the remaining ingredients; rub over both sides of fillets. Place in an ungreased 15x10x1-in. baking pan.
2. Bake, uncovered, at 350° until fish flakes easily with a fork, 10-15 minutes.
1 SERVING 259 cal., 16g fat (3g sat. fat), 80mg chol., 386mg sod., 2g carb. (0 sugars, 1g fiber), 27g pro.

LAZY LASAGNA

NAKED FISH TACOS

CHEESY HAM & POTATOES

If you love scalloped potatoes but not lots of leftovers, try this downsized recipe made in a small slow cooker.
—*Wendy Rowley, Green River, WY*

....

PREP: 20 min. • **COOK:** 5 hours
MAKES: 2 servings

2	large red potatoes, cubed
⅓	cup cubed Velveeta
¾	cup cubed fully cooked ham
1	Tbsp. dried minced onion
⅔	cup condensed cream of celery soup, undiluted
⅔	cup 2% milk
1	Tbsp. all-purpose flour
¼	tsp. pepper

1. In a greased 1½-qt. slow cooker, layer the potatoes, cheese, ham and onion.
2. In a small bowl, combine cream of celery soup and milk; whisk in flour and pepper. Pour over the potatoes. Cover and cook on low until potatoes are tender, 5-6 hours. Stir before serving.

1½ CUPS 398 cal., 15g fat (6g sat. fat), 52mg chol., 1534mg sod., 45g carb. (8g sugars, 4g fiber), 20g pro.

NAKED FISH TACOS

These just might be my husband's all-time favorite tacos. I like to serve fresh melon alongside them to balance the subtle heat of the cabbage mixture.
—*Elizabeth Bramkamp, Gig Harbor, WA*

....

TAKES: 25 min. • **MAKES:** 2 servings

1	cup coleslaw mix
¼	cup chopped fresh cilantro
1	green onion, sliced
1	tsp. chopped seeded jalapeno pepper
4	tsp. canola oil, divided
2	tsp. lime juice
½	tsp. ground cumin
½	tsp. salt, divided
¼	tsp. pepper, divided
2	tilapia fillets (6 oz. each)
½	medium ripe avocado, peeled and sliced

1. Place the first 4 ingredients in a bowl; toss with 2 tsp. canola oil, lime juice, cumin, ¼ tsp. salt and ⅛ tsp. pepper. Refrigerate until serving.
2. Pat the fillets dry with paper towels; sprinkle with remaining salt and pepper. In a large nonstick skillet, heat remaining oil over medium-high heat; cook tilapia until fish just begins to flake easily with a fork, 3-4 minutes per side. Top with slaw and sliced avocado.

1 SERVING 293 cal., 16g fat (2g sat. fat), 83mg chol., 663mg sod., 6g carb. (1g sugars, 3g fiber), 33g pro.
DIABETIC EXCHANGES 5 lean meat, 3 fat, 1 vegetable.

TEST KITCHEN TIP

....

If you're following a low-carb diet, this dish is for you! If not, pair it up with a whole grain side like brown rice pilaf or corn and pepper saute.

PAN-SEARED COD

One of the easiest recipes I've ever found for cod is also the most delicious. The fillets go wonderfully with the crunchy pine nuts, onions and cilantro.
—*Lucy Lu Wang, Seattle, WA*

....

TAKES: 25 min. • **MAKES:** 2 servings

- 2   **cod fillets (6 oz. each)**
- ½   **tsp. salt**
- ¼   **tsp. pepper**
- 3   **Tbsp. olive oil, divided**
- ½   **large sweet onion, thinly sliced**
- ½   **cup dry white wine**
- ¼   **cup coarsely chopped fresh cilantro**
- 1   **Tbsp. pine nuts or sliced almonds**

1. Pat cod dry with paper towels; sprinkle with salt and pepper. In a large nonstick skillet, heat 2 Tbsp. oil over medium-high heat. Brown fillets lightly on both sides; remove from pan.

2. In same skillet, heat the remaining oil over medium heat. Add onion; cook and stir until softened, 4-5 minutes. Stir in wine; cook until onion is lightly browned, stirring occasionally, 3-4 minutes longer. Return cod to pan. Reduce heat to low; cook, covered, until fish just begins to flake easily with a fork, 2-3 minutes.

3. Remove cod from pan. Stir cilantro and pine nuts into onion; serve with fish.

1 FILLET WITH ¼ CUP ONION MIXTURE
378 cal., 24g fat (3g sat. fat), 65mg chol., 691mg sod., 8g carb. (5g sugars, 1g fiber), 28g pro.

PAN-SEARED COD

SAUCY BEEF WITH BROCCOLI

Whenever I need a quick entree, I choose a stir-fry. My favorite combination is beef and broccoli with a garlic-ginger sauce.
—*Rosa Evans, Odessa, MO*

TAKES: 30 min. • **MAKES:** 2 servings

- 1 Tbsp. cornstarch
- ½ cup reduced-sodium beef broth
- ¼ cup sherry or additional beef broth
- 2 Tbsp. reduced-sodium soy sauce
- 1 Tbsp. brown sugar
- 1 garlic clove, minced
- 1 tsp. minced fresh gingerroot
- 2 tsp. canola oil, divided
- ½ lb. beef top sirloin steak, cut into ¼-in.-thick strips
- 2 cups fresh small broccoli florets
- 8 green onions, cut into 1-in. pieces

1. Mix the first 7 ingredients. In a large nonstick skillet, heat 1 tsp. canola oil over medium-high heat; stir-fry the beef until browned, 1-3 minutes. Remove from pan.
2. Stir-fry broccoli in the remaining oil until crisp-tender, 3-5 minutes. Add green onions; cook just until tender, 1-2 minutes. Stir cornstarch mixture and add to pan. Bring to a boil; cook and stir until the sauce is thickened, 2-3 minutes. Add beef and heat through.
1¼ CUPS 313 cal., 11g fat (3g sat. fat), 68mg chol., 816mg sod., 20g carb. (11g sugars, 4g fiber), 29g pro.
DIABETIC EXCHANGES 3 lean meat, 1 starch, 1 vegetable, 1 fat.

"Fresh ginger really adds flavor to this dish. It was very simple and is great for busy weeknights. We served it over cauliflower rice."
LPHJKITCHEN, TASTEOFHOME.COM

HERBED LEMON PORK CHOPS

You'll get rave reviews for these tender and juicy pork chops. A tongue-tingling blend of herbs and a splash of lemon pack on the flavor in just 20 minutes.
—*Billi Jo Sylvester, New Smyrna Beach, FL*

TAKES: 20 min. • **MAKES:** 2 servings

- 1 tsp. salt-free garlic seasoning blend
- ½ tsp. dried basil
- ½ tsp. dried oregano
- ½ tsp. dried parsley flakes
- ¼ tsp. salt
- ¼ tsp. dried rosemary, crushed
- ¼ tsp. garlic powder
- 2 bone-in pork loin chops (6 oz. each)
- 1 tsp. olive oil
- 1 Tbsp. lemon juice

1. Mix seasonings; rub over both sides of pork chops. In a large nonstick skillet, heat oil over medium-high heat. Add pork chops; cook until a thermometer reads 145°, 5-8 minutes per side.
2. Remove from the heat; drizzle with lemon juice. Let stand, covered, 5 minutes before serving.
1 PORK CHOP 200 cal., 10g fat (3g sat. fat), 74mg chol., 350mg sod., 1g carb. (0 sugars, 0 fiber), 26g pro.
DIABETIC EXCHANGES 4 lean meat, ½ fat.

MUSHROOM STEAK SALAD
WITH WALNUT VINAIGRETTE

MUSHROOM STEAK SALAD WITH WALNUT VINAIGRETTE

When I want to serve a romantic dinner for my husband and me, I fix an elegant green salad full of savory steak and mushrooms. Crusty French bread and a glass of wine make ideal accompaniments.
—Candace McMenamin, Lexington, SC

TAKES: 30 min. • **MAKES:** 2 servings

- 8 oz. boneless beef sirloin steak (¾ in. thick)
- 3 Tbsp. olive oil, divided
- 1 cup each sliced fresh baby portobello, shiitake and button mushrooms
- 2 Tbsp. balsamic vinegar
- 1 Tbsp. minced fresh thyme or 1 tsp. dried thyme
- 2 Tbsp. walnut oil
- 2 Tbsp. finely chopped walnuts
- 3 cups torn mixed salad greens
- 1 shallot, sliced
- 2 Tbsp. crumbled goat cheese

1. In a large skillet over medium heat, cook steak in 1 Tbsp. olive oil until meat reaches the desired doneness (for medium-rare, a thermometer should read 135°; medium, 140°; medium-well, 145°), 4-6 minutes on each side. Remove from the skillet; let stand for 5 minutes before slicing.

2. Meanwhile, in the same skillet, saute mushrooms until tender. In a small bowl, combine balsamic vinegar and thyme. Whisk in walnut oil and remaining olive oil. Stir in walnuts.

3. Divide salad greens and shallot between 2 serving bowls. Cut steak into slices. Top salads with steak and mushrooms. Drizzle with dressing; sprinkle with cheese.

1 SERVING 602 cal., 48g fat (9g sat. fat), 75mg chol., 151mg sod., 14g carb. (5g sugars, 4g fiber), 31g pro.

"This is an easy recipe for a quick dinner. I grilled the steak, which added more flavor. I also used herbed goat cheese."
JCV4, TASTEOFHOME.COM

TILAPIA WITH JASMINE RICE

This tender, flavorful tilapia paired with fragrant jasmine rice is absolutely to die for. And it gets better—each delicious serving has only 5 grams of fat!
—*Shirl Parsons, Cape Carteret, NC*

....

TAKES: 25 min. • **MAKES:** 2 servings

- ¾ cup water
- ½ cup uncooked jasmine rice
- 1½ tsp. butter
- ¼ tsp. ground cumin
- ¼ tsp. seafood seasoning
- ¼ tsp. pepper
- ⅛ tsp. salt
- 2 tilapia fillets (6 oz. each)
- ¼ cup Italian salad dressing

1. In a small saucepan, combine water, rice and butter; bring to a boil. Reduce heat; simmer, covered, until liquid is absorbed and rice is tender, 15-20 minutes.

2. Meanwhile, mix seasonings; sprinkle over tilapia. In a large skillet, heat salad dressing over medium heat until hot. Add fillets; cook until fish just begins to flake easily with a fork, 3-4 minutes per side. Serve with rice.

1 FILLET WITH ¾ CUP RICE 412 cal., 9g fat (3g sat. fat), 90mg chol., 615mg sod., 42g carb. (2g sugars, 1g fiber), 36g pro.
DIABETIC EXCHANGES 4 lean meat, 3 starch, ½ fat.

GARDEN-FRESH WHOLE WHEAT FETTUCCINE

Here's a delicious combination of whole wheat pasta and fresh garden produce. I toss it all with heart-healthy olive oil and add feta cheese to give it bite.
—*Angela Spengler, Niceville, FL*

....

TAKES: 30 min. • **MAKES:** 4 servings

- 8 oz. uncooked whole wheat fettuccine
- 2 medium ears sweet corn, husked
- 2 tsp. plus 2 Tbsp. olive oil, divided
- ½ cup chopped sweet red pepper
- 4 green onions, chopped
- 2 medium tomatoes, chopped
- ½ tsp. salt
- ½ tsp. pepper
- 1 cup crumbled feta cheese
- 2 Tbsp. minced fresh parsley

1. In a Dutch oven, cook the fettuccine according to package directions, adding corn during the last 8 minutes of cooking.

2. Meanwhile, in a small skillet, heat 2 tsp. oil over medium-high heat. Add red pepper and green onions; cook and stir until tender.

3. Drain pasta and corn; transfer pasta to a large bowl. Cool corn slightly; cut corn from cob and add to pasta. Add tomatoes, salt, pepper, remaining oil and the pepper mixture; toss to combine. Sprinkle with cheese and parsley.

2 CUPS 422 cal., 15g fat (4g sat. fat), 15mg chol., 580mg sod., 56g carb. (6g sugars, 10g fiber), 17g pro.

TILAPIA WITH JASMINE RICE

SALMON WITH SPINACH SAUCE

Poaching is a healthy way to prepare an entree as delicate as fish,keeping it moist and tender while cooking. In this recipe, a flavorful spinach sauce adds a pretty green accent to the pink salmon.
—Taste of Home *Test Kitchen*

TAKES: 20 min. • **MAKES:** 2 servings

5	oz. frozen chopped spinach, thawed and squeezed dry (about ½ cup)
⅓	cup mayonnaise
1½	tsp. Dijon mustard
1	tsp. lemon juice
⅛	tsp. garlic salt
2	salmon fillets (6 oz. each)
½	tsp. lemon-pepper seasoning
4	slices lemon

1. In a small bowl, combine the spinach, mayonnaise, Dijon mustard, lemon juice and garlic salt; cover and refrigerate until serving.

2. Place trivet insert and 1 cup water in a 3- or 6-qt. electric pressure cooker. Place fish on trivet; sprinkle with lemon pepper and top with lemon slices. Lock lid; close pressure-release valve. Adjust to pressure-cook on high for 3 minutes. Quick-release pressure. A thermometer inserted in fish should read at least 145°.

3. Discard lemon slices. Serve salmon with spinach sauce.

1 SERVING 533 cal., 43g fat (7g sat. fat), 88mg chol., 617mg sod., 4g carb. (1g sugars, 2g fiber), 32g pro.

SLOW COOKER, INSTANT POT® & AIR FRYER
FOR TWO

Pull out those small kitchen appliances
and let them do most of the work for you!
You'll discover they can be indispensable when
you're cooking for a small household.

AIR-FRYER SWEET
& SOUR PORK

AIR-FRYER SWEET & SOUR PORK

Covered with a delectable sauce and green onions, this tenderloin is a tempting entree. Round out your meal with rice and veggies.
—*Leigh Rys, Herndon, VA*

PREP: 25 min. • **COOK:** 15 min.
MAKES: 2 servings

- ½ cup unsweetened crushed pineapple, undrained
- ½ cup cider vinegar
- ¼ cup sugar
- ¼ cup packed dark brown sugar
- ¼ cup ketchup
- 1 Tbsp. reduced-sodium soy sauce
- 1½ tsp. Dijon mustard
- ½ tsp. garlic powder
- 1 pork tenderloin (¾ lb.), halved
- ⅛ tsp. salt
- ⅛ tsp. pepper
  Sliced green onions, optional
  Cooking spray

1. In a small saucepan, combine the first 8 ingredients. Bring to a boil; reduce heat. Simmer, uncovered, until thickened, 6-8 minutes, stirring occasionally.
2. Preheat air fryer to 350°. Sprinkle the pork tenderloin with salt and pepper. Place pork on greased tray in air-fryer basket; spritz with cooking spray. Cook until pork begins to brown around edges, 7-8 minutes. Turn; pour 2 Tbsp. sauce over pork. Cook until a thermometer inserted into pork reads at least 145°, 10-12 minutes longer. Let pork stand 5 minutes before slicing. Serve with remaining sauce. If desired, top with sliced green onions.

5 OZ. COOKED PORK WITH ½ CUP SAUCE 502 cal., 7g fat (2g sat. fat), 95mg chol., 985mg sod., 72g carb. (69g sugars, 1g fiber), 35g pro.

SLOW-COOKER
ITALIAN CHICKEN

SLOW-COOKER ITALIAN CHICKEN

My father used to love it when I made my Italian chicken. Featuring a flavorful tomato sauce, it's especially satisfying served over a plate of hot spaghetti.
—*Deanna D'Auria, Banning, CA*

PREP: 20 min. • **COOK:** 3 hours
MAKES: 2 servings

- 2 boneless skinless chicken breast halves (4 oz. each)
- 1 cup reduced-sodium chicken broth
- 1 cup stewed tomatoes, cut up
- ½ cup tomato sauce
- 1 small green pepper, chopped
- 1 Tbsp. chopped green onion
- 1 garlic clove, minced
- 1½ tsp. chili powder
- ½ tsp. ground mustard
- ¼ tsp. pepper
- ⅛ tsp. garlic powder
- ⅛ tsp. onion powder
- 2 Tbsp. all-purpose flour
- ¼ cup cold water
  Hot cooked pasta
  Shaved Parmesan cheese, optional

1. Place chicken in a 1½-qt. slow cooker. In a bowl, combine the broth, tomatoes, tomato sauce, green pepper, onion, garlic and seasonings; pour over chicken. Cover and cook on low until chicken is tender, 3-4 hours. Remove chicken and keep warm.
2. Pour the cooking juices into a small saucepan. Combine the flour and cold water until smooth; stir into juices. Bring to a boil; cook and stir for 1 minute or until thickened. Serve with chicken and pasta. If desired, top with Parmesan cheese.
1 SERVING 230 cal., 4g fat (1g sat. fat), 63mg chol., 900mg sod., 23g carb. (9g sugars, 4g fiber), 28g pro.

TENDER BEEF OVER NOODLES

I dress up economical beef stew meat with a sweet red sauce and serve it with noodles for a stick-to-your-ribs main dish. Just add a salad and garlic bread.

—*Olivia Gust, Salem, OR*

PREP: 15 min. • **COOK:** 5½ hours
MAKES: 2 servings

- ½ lb. beef stew meat
- ⅓ cup chopped onion
- 1 tsp. canola oil
- 1 cup water, divided
- ⅓ cup ketchup
- 1 Tbsp. brown sugar
- 1 Tbsp. Worcestershire sauce
- ½ tsp. paprika
- ¼ tsp. ground mustard
- 3 Tbsp. all-purpose flour
- 1 cup uncooked egg noodles
  Minced fresh parsley, optional

1. In a small skillet, brown beef stew meat and onion in oil; drain. Transfer to a 1½-qt. slow cooker.
2. In a small bowl, combine ½ cup water, ketchup, brown sugar, Worcestershire sauce, paprika and mustard; pour over meat. Cover and cook on low until meat is tender, about 5 hours.
3. Combine the flour and remaining water until smooth; stir into the meat mixture. Cover and cook until thickened, about 30 minutes longer.
4. Meanwhile, cook egg noodles according to package directions; drain. Stir in parsley if desired. Serve with beef.

1½ CUPS 385 cal., 11g fat (3g sat. fat), 89mg chol., 611mg sod., 44g carb. (13g sugars, 2g fiber), 27g pro.

SIMPLE CHICKEN STEW

Slow-cooker recipes just don't get much easier than this one. It was an experiment of my husband's and quickly became our favorite Sunday dinner.

—*Amy Dulling, Rockwood, TN*

PREP: 20 min. • **COOK:** 6 hours
MAKES: 2 servings

- 1 can (10¾ oz.) condensed cream of chicken soup, undiluted
- 1 cup water
- ½ lb. boneless skinless chicken breast, cubed
- 1 large potato, peeled and cubed
- 2 medium carrots, sliced
- ½ cup sliced fresh mushrooms
- ¼ cup chopped onion
- 1 tsp. chicken bouillon granules
- ¼ tsp. poultry seasoning

1. In a 1½-qt. slow cooker, combine all of the ingredients.
2. Cover and cook on low for 6-7 hours or until chicken and vegetables are tender.

1½ CUPS 427 cal., 6g fat (2g sat. fat), 75mg chol., 834mg sod., 62g carb. (11g sugars, 6g fiber), 30g pro.

TENDER BEEF OVER NOODLES

PRESSURE-COOKER
MEXICAN STUFFED PEPPERS

PRESSURE-COOKER
MEXICAN STUFFED PEPPERS

Give stuffed peppers a southwestern twist!
The spiced-up filling is so good. I've even
used it to make a meat loaf that we eat not
only hot, but also cold in sandwiches with
cheese, mayo and salsa.
—*Traci Wynne, Denver, PA*

PREP: 20 min. • **COOK:** 15 min. + releasing
MAKES: 2 servings

- 2 medium sweet red, orange and/or
  yellow peppers
- 1 large egg, beaten
- ½ cup crushed tortilla chips
- ½ cup salsa
- ¼ cup finely chopped onion
- 2 Tbsp. minced fresh cilantro
- ½ tsp. ground cumin
- ½ tsp. seeded and finely chopped
  red chili pepper
- ¼ tsp. minced garlic
- ¼ lb. lean ground beef (90% lean)
- ¼ cup shredded Mexican cheese blend
  Sour cream

1. Place trivet insert and 1 cup water
in a 3- or 6-qt. electric pressure cooker.
2. Cut and discard the tops from peppers;
remove seeds. In a small bowl, combine the
egg, chips, salsa, onion, cilantro, cumin,
chili pepper and garlic. Crumble beef over
mixture and mix well; spoon into peppers.
Set peppers on trivet.
3. Lock lid; close pressure-release valve.
Adjust to pressure-cook on high for
12 minutes. Let pressure release naturally.
Sprinkle peppers with cheese. Serve with
sour cream and, if desired, additional salsa.
1 STUFFED PEPPER 319 cal., 15g fat (5g sat.
fat), 141mg chol., 458mg sod., 25g carb. (8g
sugars, 4g fiber), 20g pro.

AIR-FRYER COCONUT SHRIMP
WITH APRICOT SAUCE

Coconut and panko crumbs create the
delightfully crunchy coating on this zippy
air-fryer shrimp. Keep it in mind for both
an entree and an appetizer.
—*Debi Mitchell, Flower Mound, TX*

TAKES: 30 min. • **MAKES:** 2 servings

- ½ lb. uncooked large shrimp
- ½ cup sweetened shredded coconut
- 3 Tbsp. panko bread crumbs
- 2 large egg whites
- ⅛ tsp. salt
  Dash pepper
  Dash Louisiana-style hot sauce
- 3 Tbsp. all-purpose flour

SAUCE
- ⅓ cup apricot preserves
- ½ tsp. cider vinegar
  Dash crushed red pepper flakes

1. Preheat air fryer to 375°. Peel and devein
shrimp, leaving tails on.
2. In a shallow bowl, toss coconut with
bread crumbs. In another shallow bowl,
whisk egg whites, salt, pepper and hot
sauce. Place flour in a third shallow bowl.
3. Dip the shrimp in flour to coat lightly;
shake off excess. Dip in egg white mixture,
then in coconut mixture, patting to help
coating adhere.
4. Place shrimp in a single layer on greased
tray in air-fryer basket. Cook 4 minutes;
turn shrimp and continue cooking until
coconut is lightly browned and shrimp turn
pink, another 4 minutes.
5. Meanwhile, combine sauce ingredients
in a small saucepan; cook and stir over
medium-low heat until apricot preserves
are melted. Serve shrimp immediately with
the sauce.
6 SHRIMP WITH 2 TBSP. SAUCE 423 cal.,
10g fat (8g sat. fat), 138mg chol., 440mg
sod., 59g carb. (34g sugars, 2g fiber),
25g pro.

SWEET ONION & CHERRY PORK CHOPS

When I want to get a jump on dinner, I often turn to these tender pork chops. The sweet and savory cherry sauce really sets them apart. Try a wild rice pilaf on the side.
—*Stephanie Ray, Naples, FL*

PREP: 15 min. • **COOK:** 3 hours
MAKES: 2 servings

- ½ cup fresh or frozen pitted tart cherries, thawed
- 2 Tbsp. chopped sweet onion
- 1 Tbsp. honey
- ½ tsp. seasoned salt
- ¼ tsp. pepper
- 2 boneless pork loin chops (5 oz. each)
- 1 tsp. cornstarch
- 1 tsp. cold water

1. In a 1½-qt. slow cooker, combine the first 5 ingredients; top with pork chops. Cover and cook on low until the meat is tender, 3-4 hours.

2. Remove the meat to a serving platter; keep warm. Skim fat from cooking juices; transfer to a small saucepan. Bring liquid to a boil. Combine cornstarch and cold water until smooth. Gradually stir into pan. Bring to a boil; cook and stir until thickened, about 2 minutes. Serve with meat.

1 PORK CHOP WITH ¼ CUP CHERRY MIXTURE 278 cal., 8g fat (3g sat. fat), 68mg chol., 425mg sod., 23g carb. (9g sugars, 1g fiber), 28g pro. **DIABETIC EXCHANGES** 4 lean meat, 1 starch, ½ fat.

ROSEMARY POT ROAST

A neighbor shared her favorite pot roast recipe with me. I'm so glad she did! It's such a treat when I come home to a slow cooker filled with this comforting, ready-to-eat meal. The aroma draws you to the kitchen as soon as you walk in the door.
—*Marcia Schroeder, River Edge, NJ*

PREP: 15 min. • **COOK:** 8 hours
MAKES: 2 servings

- 1 boneless beef chuck steak (¾ in. thick and ¾ lb.)
- 1 to 2 tsp. canola oil
- ¼ cup beef broth
- ¼ cup tomato sauce
- ¼ cup dry red wine or additional beef broth
- 2 Tbsp. chopped onion
- 1 garlic clove, minced
- 1½ tsp. dried parsley flakes
- ¼ tsp. minced fresh rosemary
- ⅛ tsp. salt
- ⅛ tsp. pepper
- 1½ tsp. cornstarch
- 1 Tbsp. water

1. In a large skillet, brown the beef in oil on both sides. Transfer to a 1½-qt. slow cooker. In a small bowl, combine the broth, tomato sauce, wine, onion, garlic, parsley, rosemary, salt and pepper; pour over beef. Cover and cook on low until meat is tender, about 8 hours.

2. Remove beef and keep warm. In a small saucepan, combine cornstarch and water until smooth; stir in cooking juices. Bring to a boil; cook and stir until thickened, about 2 minutes. Serve with beef.

5 OZ. COOKED BEEF 358 cal., 19g fat (6g sat. fat), 111mg chol., 472mg sod., 6g carb. (1g sugars, 1g fiber), 34g pro.

TEST KITCHEN TIPS

Mashed potatoes and steamed broccoli with lemon butter make this a hearty meal for two. Also, leftovers are so tender and tasty, you just might want to double this recipe to serve over noodles or in sandwiches the next day.

TROPICAL BBQ CHICKEN

TROPICAL BBQ CHICKEN

Like chicken but want to fix it in a new way?
Here's one of my top choices. The delicious,
slightly spicy sauce is sure to win you over.
—*Yvonne McKim, Vancouver, WA*

PREP: 15 min. • **COOK:** 3 hours
MAKES: 2 servings

- 2 chicken leg quarters (8 oz. each),
  skin removed
- 3 Tbsp. ketchup
- 2 Tbsp. orange juice
- 1 Tbsp. brown sugar
- 1 Tbsp. red wine vinegar
- 1 Tbsp. olive oil
- 1 tsp. minced fresh parsley
- ½ tsp. Worcestershire sauce
- ¼ tsp. garlic salt
- ⅛ tsp. pepper
- 2 tsp. cornstarch
- 1 Tbsp. cold water

1. With a sharp knife, cut leg quarters at
the joints if desired; place in a 1½-qt. slow
cooker. In a small bowl, combine ketchup,
orange juice, brown sugar, vinegar, oil,
parsley, Worcestershire sauce, garlic salt
and pepper; pour over chicken.
2. Cover and cook on low until the meat
is tender, 3-4 hours.
3. Remove chicken to a serving platter;
keep warm.
4. Skim fat from cooking juices; transfer
½ cup to a small saucepan. Bring liquid to
a boil. Combine cornstarch and water until
smooth. Gradually stir into pan. Bring to
a boil; cook and stir until thickened, about
2 minutes. Serve with chicken. If desired,
top with additional fresh parsley.
1 SERVING 301 cal., 14g fat (3g sat. fat),
83mg chol., 601mg sod., 18g carb. (14g
sugars, 0 fiber), 25g pro.

PRESSURE-COOKER
PORK RIBS

PRESSURE-COOKER PORK RIBS

When I was younger, my mother prepared these lip-smacking ribs for special Saturday dinners. Now I can enjoy this treat anytime with the help of a pressure cooker.
—Paula Zsiray, Logan, UT

....

PREP: 25 min. • **COOK:** 20 min. + releasing
MAKES: 2 servings

- 1 lb. boneless country-style pork ribs, cut into 2-in. chunks
- ½ tsp. onion salt
- ½ tsp. pepper
- ½ tsp. paprika
- 2 tsp. canola oil
- 1 cup water
- 2 Tbsp. ketchup
- 2 tsp. white vinegar
- ½ tsp. Worcestershire sauce
- ½ tsp. prepared mustard
- ⅛ tsp. celery seed

1. Sprinkle ribs with onion salt, pepper and paprika. Select saute setting on a 3- or 6-qt. electric pressure cooker. Adjust for medium heat; add oil. When oil is hot, brown meat on all sides; remove from pressure cooker.

Add the water to pressure cooker. Cook 30 seconds, stirring to loosen browned bits from the pan. Press cancel. Whisk in the remaining ingredients. Return ribs to pressure cooker.

2. Lock lid; close pressure-release valve. Adjust to pressure-cook on high for 20 minutes. Let pressure release naturally. If desired, skim the fat and thicken the cooking juices.

6 OZ. COOKED PORK 417 cal., 26g fat (8g sat. fat), 131mg chol., 764mg sod., 5g carb. (4g sugars, 0 fiber), 40g pro.

RICH & CREAMY POTATO SOUP

Every year for St. Patrick's Day, I serve up brimming bowls of potato soup. We always look forward to it.
—Mary Jo O'Brien, Hastings, MN

....

PREP: 30 min. • **COOK:** 5 hours
MAKES: 2 servings

- 2¾ cups cubed peeled potatoes, divided
- 1⅓ cups water
- 2 Tbsp. butter, cubed
- ⅔ cup cubed fully cooked ham
- 1 celery rib, chopped
- ⅓ cup chopped onion
- ¼ tsp. garlic powder
- ¼ tsp. paprika
  Dash pepper
- ¼ lb. Velveeta, cubed
- ⅓ cup sour cream
  Whole milk, optional

1. Place 2 cups potatoes in a saucepan; add the water. Bring to a boil. Reduce heat; cover and cook for 10-15 minutes or until tender. Remove from the heat (do not drain). Mash potatoes; stir in butter.

2. In a 1½-qt. slow cooker, combine the ham, celery, onion, garlic powder, paprika, pepper and remaining cubed potatoes. Stir in mashed potatoes; top with cheese. Cover and cook on low for 5-6 hours or until vegetables are tender. Stir in the sour cream until blended. Thin soup with milk if desired.

1½ CUPS 643 cal., 37g fat (22g sat. fat), 127mg chol., 1436mg sod., 53g carb. (9g sugars, 5g fiber), 25g pro.

CHIPOTLE-ORANGE CHICKEN

Big on flavor and easy on your schedule, this recipe includes directions for freezing. I like to have a side of rice to soak up every last drop of the delectable sauce.
—*Cittie, TasteofHome.com*

PREP: 15 min. • **COOK:** 3 hours
MAKES: 2 servings

- 2 boneless skinless chicken breast halves (6 oz. each)
- ⅛ tsp. salt
  Dash pepper
- ¼ cup chicken broth
- 3 Tbsp. orange marmalade
- 1½ tsp. canola oil
- 1½ tsp. balsamic vinegar
- 1½ tsp. minced chipotle pepper in adobo sauce
- 1½ tsp. honey
- ½ tsp. chili powder
- ⅛ tsp. garlic powder
- 2 tsp. cornstarch
- 1 Tbsp. cold water

Sprinkle chicken with salt and pepper. Transfer to a 1½-qt. slow cooker. In a small bowl, combine the broth, marmalade, oil, vinegar, chipotle pepper, honey, chili powder and garlic powder; pour mixture over chicken. Cover and cook on low for 3-4 hours or until a thermometer reads 165°. Remove chicken to a serving platter and keep warm. Place cooking juices in a small saucepan; bring to a boil. Combine cornstarch and water until smooth. Gradually stir into the pan. Bring to a boil; cook and stir until thickened, about 2 minutes. Serve sauce with chicken.

FREEZE OPTION Cool chicken mixture. Freeze in freezer containers. To use, partially thaw in the refrigerator overnight. Heat through slowly in a covered skillet until a thermometer inserted in chicken reads 165°, stirring occasionally; add broth or water if necessary.

1 CHICKEN BREAST HALF 324 cal., 8g fat (1g sat. fat), 95mg chol., 414mg sod., 29g carb. (24g sugars, 1g fiber), 35g pro.

POLISH KRAUT WITH APPLES

This combination of apples, sauerkraut and smoked sausage brings Old World appeal to the table. I toss everything into the slow cooker, then just dig in at dinnertime.
—*Caren Markee, Cary, IL*

PREP: 10 min. • **COOK:** 3 hours
MAKES: 2 servings

- 1 cup sauerkraut, rinsed and well drained
- ½ lb. smoked Polish sausage or kielbasa, cut up
- 1 large tart apple, peeled and cut into eighths
- ¼ cup packed brown sugar
- ¼ tsp. caraway seeds, optional
  Dash pepper
- ⅓ cup apple juice

1. Place half of sauerkraut in an ungreased 1½-qt. slow cooker. Top with the sausage, apples, brown sugar, caraway seeds if desired and pepper. Top with remaining sauerkraut. Pour apple juice over all.
2. Cover and cook on low until apples are tender, 3-4 hours.
1 CUP 522 cal., 30g fat (10g sat. fat), 81mg chol., 1440mg sod., 49g carb. (41g sugars, 3g fiber), 15g pro.

CHIPOTLE-ORANGE CHICKEN

SLOW-COOKER VEGGIE LASAGNA

APRICOT-ORANGE SALSA CHICKEN

Sweet oranges and apricots blend perfectly with the zippy salsa in this five-ingredient entree. Served over rice, it's a dinner we've enjoyed time and again.
—*LaDonna Reed, Ponca City, OK*

....

PREP: 10 min. • **COOK:** 2½ hours
MAKES: 2 servings

- ¾ cup salsa
- ⅓ cup apricot preserves
- ¼ cup orange juice
- 2 boneless skinless chicken breast halves (5 oz. each)
- 1 cup hot cooked rice

1. In a small bowl, combine salsa, apricot preserves and orange juice. In a 1½-qt. slow cooker coated with cooking spray, layer ⅓ cup salsa mixture and a chicken breast. Repeat layers. Top with remaining salsa mixture.
2. Cover and cook on low until chicken is tender, 2½-3 hours. If desired, thicken pan juices. Serve with rice.
1 CHICKEN BREAST HALF WITH ½ CUP RICE 427 cal., 4g fat (1g sat. fat), 78mg chol., 450mg sod., 66g carb. (25g sugars, 0 fiber), 31g pro.

MAPLE PORK RIBS

A luscious maple-mustard sauce will take your next plate of ribs to a new level.
—*Phyllis Schmalz, Kansas City, KS*

....

PREP: 10 min. • **COOK:** 5 hours
MAKES: 2 servings

- 1 lb. boneless country-style pork ribs, trimmed and cut into 3-in. pieces
- 2 tsp. canola oil
- 1 medium onion, sliced and separated into rings
- 3 Tbsp. maple syrup
- 2 Tbsp. spicy brown or Dijon mustard

In a large skillet, brown the ribs in oil on all sides; drain. Place ribs and onion in a 1½-qt. slow cooker. Combine syrup and mustard; pour over ribs. Cover and cook on low until meat is tender, 5-6 hours.
4 OZ. COOKED PORK 428 cal., 20g fat (6g sat. fat), 98mg chol., 272mg sod., 27g carb. (24g sugars, 2g fiber), 31g pro.

SLOW-COOKER VEGGIE LASAGNA

Lasagna in a slow cooker? You bet! Here's a veggie-licious version that pleases even the meat lovers.
—*Laura Davister, Little Suamico, WI*

....

PREP: 25 min. • **COOK:** 3½ hours
MAKES: 2 servings

- ½ cup shredded part-skim mozzarella cheese
- 3 Tbsp. 1% cottage cheese
- 2 Tbsp. grated Parmesan cheese
- 2 Tbsp. egg substitute
- ½ tsp. Italian seasoning
- ⅛ tsp. garlic powder
- ¾ cup meatless spaghetti sauce
- ½ cup sliced zucchini
- 2 no-cook lasagna noodles
- 4 cups fresh baby spinach
- ½ cup sliced fresh mushrooms

1. Cut two 18x3-in. strips of heavy-duty foil; crisscross strips so they resemble an "X." Place strips on the bottom and up the sides of a 1½-qt. slow cooker. Coat strips with cooking spray.
2. In a small bowl, combine the first 6 ingredients. Spread 1 Tbsp. spaghetti sauce on the bottom of prepared slow cooker. Top with half of the zucchini and a third of the cheese mixture.
3. Break noodles into 1-in. pieces; sprinkle half of the noodles over cheese mixture. Spread with 1 Tbsp. sauce. Top with half of the spinach and half of the mushrooms. Repeat layers. Top with remaining cheese mixture and spaghetti sauce.
4. Cover and cook on low for 3½-4 hours or until noodles are tender.
1 PIECE 249 cal., 7g fat (4g sat. fat), 22mg chol., 792mg sod., 28g carb. (10g sugars, 4g fiber), 19g pro.
DIABETIC EXCHANGES 2 medium-fat meat, 1½ starch, 1 vegetable.

APRICOT-ORANGE
SALSA CHICKEN

STRAWBERRY PRETZEL DESSERT

Sliced berries and gelatin top the smooth cream cheese filling and crispy pretzel crust in this sweet-salty layered dessert. I think it's best eaten within a day of being made.
—*Wendy Weaver, Leetonia, OH*

PREP: 15 min. + chilling • **MAKES:** 2 servings

- ⅓ cup crushed pretzels
- 2 Tbsp. butter, softened
- 2 oz. cream cheese, softened
- ¼ cup sugar
- ¾ cup whipped topping
- 2 Tbsp. plus 1½ tsp. strawberry gelatin
- ½ cup boiling water
- 1 cup sliced fresh strawberries
  Optional: Whipped topping and pretzel twists

1. Preheat oven to 375°. In a large bowl, combine the pretzels and butter. Press onto the bottom of 2 greased 10-oz. custard cups. Bake until set, 6-8 minutes. Cool on a wire rack.

2. In a small bowl, combine cream cheese and sugar until smooth. Fold in whipped topping. Spoon over crust. Refrigerate for 30 minutes.

3. Meanwhile, in a small bowl, dissolve the strawberry gelatin in boiling water. Cover and refrigerate for 20 minutes or until slightly thickened. Fold in berries. Carefully spoon over the filling. Cover and refrigerate for at least 3 hours. If desired, top with whipped topping and pretzel twists.

1 SERVING 516 cal., 27g fat (18g sat. fat), 62mg chol., 458mg sod., 64g carb. (47g sugars, 2g fiber), 6g pro.

DESSERTS
FOR TWO

Love a luscious finale after a hearty meal?
Whether served at a celebration or a cozy
night in, the sweet delights in this chapter
fit perfectly at any table for two.

APPLE CRISP

APPLE CRISP

Here's a wonderful recipe for fall or any time of year. We like the yummy crisp best served warm from the oven with vanilla ice cream or whipped cream on top.
—*Patricia Gross, Etna Green, IN*

PREP: 10 min. • **BAKE:** 45 min.
MAKES: 2 servings

- 1 large tart apple, peeled and sliced
- 1 Tbsp. lemon juice
- 2 Tbsp. brown sugar
- 2 Tbsp. quick-cooking oats
- 2 Tbsp. butter, melted
  Dash ground cinnamon
  Whipped cream or vanilla ice cream, optional

1. Preheat oven to 350°. Place cut apples in an ungreased 2-cup baking dish; sprinkle with lemon juice. Combine brown sugar, oats, butter and cinnamon; sprinkle over the apples.
2. Cover and bake 30 minutes. Uncover; bake until the apples are tender, about 15 minutes longer. If desired, serve with whipped cream or ice cream.
1 SERVING 218 cal., 12g fat (7g sat. fat), 31mg chol., 121mg sod., 29g carb. (23g sugars, 2g fiber), 1g pro.

PUMPKIN PUDDING DESSERTS

One of the joys of autumn is cooking with pumpkin. Blending it into a pudding with cinnamon and ginger creates a seasonal treat we always look forward to.
—*Stephanie Carley, Dodgeville, WI*

TAKES: 10 min. • **MAKES:** 2 servings

- ¾ cup canned pumpkin
- ½ tsp. ground cinnamon
- ¼ tsp. ground ginger
- ¾ cup cold 2% milk
- 1 pkg. (3.3 oz.) instant white chocolate pudding mix
- ¼ cup whipped topping

1. In a small bowl, whisk the pumpkin, cinnamon and ginger. Add the milk and pudding mix; whisk for 2 minutes (mixture will be thick).
2. Transfer to individual serving dishes. Refrigerate until serving. Garnish servings with whipped topping.
1 SERVING 279 cal., 4g fat (3g sat. fat), 7mg chol., 724mg sod., 57g carb. (52g sugars, 4g fiber), 5g pro.

SPICED CHOCOLATE MOLTEN CAKES

SPICED CHOCOLATE MOLTEN CAKES

Take some time to linger over this decadent dessert. Each from-scratch mini chocolate cake promises a hint of spice and a warm, melted filling in the center. To me, there's no better ending for dinner.
—*Deb Carpenter, Hastings, MI*

TAKES: 30 min. • **MAKES:** 2 servings

- ¼ cup butter, cubed
- 2 oz. semisweet chocolate, chopped
- 1½ tsp. dry red wine
- ½ tsp. vanilla extract
- 1 large egg, room temperature
- 2 tsp. egg yolk
- ½ cup confectioners' sugar
- 3 Tbsp. all-purpose flour
- ⅛ tsp. ground cinnamon
- ⅛ tsp. ground ginger
  Additional confectioners' sugar

1. Preheat oven to 425°. In a microwave, melt the butter and chocolate; stir until smooth. Stir in wine and vanilla.
2. In a small bowl, beat the egg, egg yolk and confectioners' sugar until thick and lemon-colored. Beat in flour, ginger and cinnamon until well blended. Gradually beat in butter mixture.
3. Transfer to 2 greased 6-oz. ramekins or custard cups. Place ramekins on a baking sheet. Bake until a thermometer inserted in the center reads 160° and sides of cakes are set, 10-12 minutes.
4. Remove from oven and let stand for 1 minute. Run a knife around the edges of ramekins; invert onto dessert plates. Dust with additional confectioners' sugar. Serve immediately.
1 CAKE 560 cal., 36g fat (21g sat. fat), 234mg chol., 200mg sod., 56g carb. (43g sugars, 2g fiber), 8g pro.

LAYERED CHOCOLATE PUDDING DESSERT

These individual treats are cool, smooth, chocolaty and popular with everyone who tries them. What's not to like?
—Carma Blosser, Livermore, CO

PREP: 30 min. + cooling • **MAKES:** 2 servings

- ⅓ cup all-purpose flour
- 3 Tbsp. chopped pecans
- 3 Tbsp. butter, melted
- 3 oz. cream cheese, softened
- ⅓ cup confectioners' sugar
- 1 cup whipped topping, divided
- ⅔ cup cold 2% milk
- 3 Tbsp. instant chocolate pudding mix

1. In a small bowl, combine the flour, pecans and butter; press into 2 ungreased 8-oz. ramekins. Bake at 350° until the crust is lightly browned, 10-12 minutes. Cool on a wire rack.

2. In a small bowl, beat the cream cheese and confectioners' sugar until smooth; fold in ½ cup whipped topping. Spread over the crust.

3. In a small bowl, whisk milk and pudding mix for 2 minutes. Let stand until soft-set, about 2 minutes. Spread over cream cheese mixture. Spread with remaining whipped topping. Chill until serving.

1 SERVING 584 cal., 33g fat (19g sat. fat), 52mg chol., 264mg sod., 66g carb. (40g sugars, 2g fiber), 6g pro.

THIN MINT MILK SHAKE

Save a sleeve of chocolate-mint Girl Scout cookies to blend into creamy milk shakes. They go over big with kids and adults alike.
—Shauna Sever, San Francisco, CA

TAKES: 5 min. • **MAKES:** 2 servings

- 3 Tbsp. creme de menthe or 3 Tbsp. 2% milk plus a dash of peppermint extract
- 1¼ to 1½ cups vanilla ice cream
- 7 Girl Scout Thin Mint cookies
  Green food coloring, optional

Place all ingredients in a blender in order listed; cover and process until blended. Serve immediately.

⅔ CUP 363 cal., 12g fat (7g sat. fat), 36mg chol., 70mg sod., 49g carb. (47g sugars, 1g fiber), 3g pro.

LAYERED CHOCOLATE PUDDING DESSERT

**COCOA MERINGUES
WITH BERRIES**

🍎 **COCOA MERINGUES WITH BERRIES**

If it's too humid out to make meringues, buy them at your favorite bakery. Spoon on this sweet sauce, and you're all set!
—*Raymonde Bourgeois, Swastika, ON*

PREP: 20 min. • **BAKE:** 50 min. + standing
MAKES: 2 servings

- 1 large egg white
- ⅛ tsp. cream of tartar
  Dash salt
- 3 Tbsp. sugar, divided
- 1 Tbsp. baking cocoa
- ¼ tsp. vanilla extract
- 2 Tbsp. finely chopped
  bittersweet chocolate

BERRY SAUCE

- 2 Tbsp. sugar
- 1 tsp. cornstarch
- 2 Tbsp. orange juice
- 1 Tbsp. water
- ½ cup fresh or frozen
  blueberries, thawed
- ½ cup fresh or frozen
  raspberries, thawed
  Grated orange zest, optional

1. Place egg white in a small bowl; let stand at room temperature for 30 minutes.
2. Preheat oven to 275°. Add the cream of tartar and salt; beat on medium speed until soft peaks form. Gradually beat in 2 Tbsp. sugar.
3. Combine cocoa and remaining sugar; add to meringue with vanilla. Beat on high until stiff glossy peaks form and sugar is dissolved. Fold in chopped chocolate.
4. Drop 2 mounds onto parchment-lined baking sheet. Shape into 3-in. cups with the back of a spoon. Bake until set and dry, 50-60 minutes. Turn oven off; leave meringues in oven for 1 hour.
5. In a small saucepan, combine sugar, cornstarch, orange juice and water. Bring to a boil; cook and stir 1 minute or until thickened. Remove from heat; stir in the berries. Cool to room temperature. Spoon into meringues. If desired, top with grated orange zest.
1 MERINGUE WITH ½ CUP SAUCE 215 cal., 4g fat (2g sat. fat), 0 chol., 102mg sod., 46g carb. (41g sugars, 3g fiber), 3g pro.

CHERRY-CHOCOLATE PUDGY PIE

Here's an ooey-gooey delight for your campfires and cookouts. Yum!
—*Josh Carter, Birmingham, AL*

TAKES: 10 min. • **MAKES:** 1 serving

- 2 slices white bread
- 3 Tbsp. cherry pie filling
- 1 Tbsp. chopped almonds
- 1 Tbsp. semisweet chocolate chips

1. Place 1 slice of bread in a greased sandwich iron. Spread with cherry pie filling; top with almonds, chocolate chips and remaining bread slice. Close iron.
2. Cook over a hot campfire until golden brown and heated through, 3-6 minutes, turning occasionally.
1 SANDWICH 309 cal., 9g fat (3g sat. fat), 0 chol., 294mg sod., 51g carb. (9g sugars, 3g fiber), 7g pro.

RASPBERRY ICE CREAM IN A BAG

Making homemade ice cream is fun for the whole family. Kids can shake the bags until the liquid changes to ice cream, then enjoy the sweet reward. Fresh raspberries add great summertime flavor.
—Erin Hoffman, Canby, MN

....

TAKES: 15 min. • **MAKES:** 1 cup

- 1 cup half-and-half cream
- ½ cup fresh raspberries
- ¼ cup sugar
- 2 Tbsp. evaporated milk
- 1 tsp. vanilla extract
- 4 cups coarsely crushed ice
- ¾ cup salt

1. Using two 1-qt. resealable plastic bags, place 1 bag inside the other. Place the first 5 ingredients inside the inner bag. Seal both bags, pressing out as much air as possible.
2. Place the 2 bags in a gallon-size plastic freezer bag. Add ice and salt. Seal bag, again pressing out as much air as possible.
3. Shake and knead cream mixture until thickened, about 5 minutes. (If desired, wear mittens or wrap bags in a kitchen towel while shaking to protect hands from the cold ice.)
½ CUP 299 cal., 13g fat (9g sat. fat), 65mg chol., 76mg sod., 35g carb. (32g sugars, 2g fiber), 5g pro.

PERSIAN POACHED PEARS

These dressed-up pears are a dramatic way to finish off a Middle Eastern feast. They're delicious, fragrant and a distinctive twist on basic poached pears.
—Trisha Kruse, Eagle, ID

....

PREP: 15 min. • **COOK:** 50 min. + chilling
MAKES: 2 servings

- 2 medium firm pears
- 1 vanilla bean
- 2¼ cups water
- ½ cup white grape juice
- 2 dried apricots, chopped
- 1 Tbsp. sugar
- 1 Tbsp. honey
- 1 lemon zest strip
- 1 whole clove
- 2 Tbsp. chopped almonds, toasted

1. Core pears from the bottom, leaving stems intact. Peel pears; cut ¼ in. from the bottom of each to level if necessary. Split vanilla bean and scrape seeds; set aside.
2. In a small saucepan, combine the water, white grape juice, dried apricots, sugar, honey, lemon strip, clove, vanilla bean and seeds. Bring to a boil. Reduce heat; place pears on their sides in saucepan and poach, uncovered, for 18-22 minutes or until pears are almost tender, basting occasionally with poaching liquid.
3. Remove the pears and apricots with a slotted spoon; cool slightly. Cover and refrigerate. Bring the poaching liquid to a boil; cook until liquid is reduced to ¼ cup. Discard the vanilla bean, lemon strip and clove. Cover and refrigerate for at least 1 hour.
4. Place pears on dessert plates. Drizzle with poaching liquid. Sprinkle with apricots and almonds.
1 SERVING 258 cal., 4g fat (0 sat. fat), 0 chol., 6mg sod., 56g carb. (44g sugars, 7g fiber), 3g pro.

OLD-FASHIONED RICE PUDDING

I was fortunate to grow up around fabulous cooks. My mother and grandmother taught me to experiment with recipes, and we tried many variations of this rice pudding. It was always yummy. Now it brings back fond memories whenever I make it.
—*Laura German, North Brookfield, MA*

TAKES: 25 min. • **MAKES:** 2 servings

- 1 cup cooked long grain rice
- 1 cup whole milk
- 5 tsp. sugar
  Dash salt
- ½ tsp. vanilla extract
  Optional toppings: Whipped cream, sliced almonds, raisins, ground cinnamon and cinnamon stick

In a small heavy saucepan, combine rice, milk, sugar and salt; bring to a boil over medium heat. Reduce heat to maintain a low simmer. Cook, uncovered, until thickened, about 20 minutes, stirring often. Remove from the heat; stir in vanilla. Spoon into serving dishes. Serve warm or cold; serve with desired toppings.

1 SERVING 220 cal., 4g fat (3g sat. fat), 17mg chol., 134mg sod., 38g carb. (16g sugars, 0 fiber), 6g pro.

TEST KITCHEN TIP

For a decadent treat, substitute dried cherries for the raisins and add a swirl of chocolate syrup.

OLD-FASHIONED RICE PUDDING

BANANAS FOSTER
SUNDAES

CHERRY CREAM CHEESE TARTS

These little tarts require just five ingredients and 10 minutes of prep. If you like, replace the cherry pie filling with a different kind.
—*Cindi Mitchell, Waring, TX*

....

TAKES: 10 min. • **MAKES:** 2 servings

- 3 oz. cream cheese, softened
- ¼ cup confectioners' sugar
- ⅛ to ¼ tsp. almond or vanilla extract
- 2 individual graham cracker shells
- ¼ cup cherry pie filling

In a small bowl, beat cream cheese, sugar and extract until smooth. Spoon into shells. Top with pie filling. Refrigerate until serving.
1 TART 362 cal., 20g fat (10g sat. fat), 43mg chol., 265mg sod., 42g carb. (29g sugars, 1g fiber), 4g pro.
DIABETIC EXCHANGES 2 starch, 2 fat, 1½ fruit.

🍎 BANANAS FOSTER SUNDAES

I have fond memories of eating bananas Foster in New Orleans, and as a dietitian, I wanted to have a healthier version of that southern treat. When I couldn't find just the right recipe, I combined the best of two and added my own tweaks until I came up with a lighter variation I was happy with. It's all the yum without the guilt!
—*Lisa Varner, El Paso, TX*

....

TAKES: 15 min. • **MAKES:** 2 servings

- 1 tsp. butter
- 1 Tbsp. brown sugar
- 1 tsp. orange juice
- ⅛ tsp. ground cinnamon
- ⅛ tsp. ground nutmeg
- 1 large banana, sliced
- 2 tsp. chopped pecans, toasted
- ⅛ tsp. rum extract
- 1 cup reduced-fat vanilla ice cream

In a large nonstick skillet, melt butter over medium-low heat. Stir in the brown sugar, orange juice, cinnamon and nutmeg until blended. Add the banana and pecans; cook until banana is glazed and slightly softened, stirring lightly, 2-3 minutes. Remove from heat; stir in extract. Serve with ice cream.
1 SUNDAE 259 cal., 8g fat (4g sat. fat), 26mg chol., 74mg sod., 45g carb. (32g sugars, 2g fiber), 5g pro.

LEMON PUDDING CAKE

My husband loves this because it tastes like lemon meringue pie. The cake is no-fuss and makes just enough for the two of us.
—*Dawn Fagerstrom, Warren, MN*

....

PREP: 15 min. • **BAKE:** 40 min.
MAKES: 2 servings

- 1 large egg, separated, room temperature
- ½ cup sugar
- ⅓ cup whole milk
- 2 Tbsp. all-purpose flour
- 2 Tbsp. lemon juice
- 1 tsp. grated lemon zest
- ⅛ tsp. salt
  Optional: Confectioners' sugar, Whipped cream, and lemon slices

1. Preheat oven to 325°. In a bowl, beat egg yolk. Add sugar, milk, flour, lemon juice, zest and salt; beat until smooth. Beat egg white until stiff peaks form; gently fold into the lemon mixture. Pour into 2 ungreased 6-oz. custard cups (cups will be very full).
2. Place the cups in an 8-in. square baking pan. Pour boiling water into the pan to a depth of 1 in. Bake until a knife inserted in the center comes out clean and the top is golden, 40-45 minutes. If desired, top with confectioners' sugar, lemon slices and whipped cream.
1 SERVING 288 cal., 4g fat (2g sat. fat), 112mg chol., 200mg sod., 60g carb. (51g sugars, 0 fiber), 5g pro.

LEMON PUDDING CAKE

SEMISWEET CHOCOLATE MOUSSE

As soon as I tried my friend's rich, velvety chocolate mousse, I had a new favorite dessert. Garnishing it with berries and whipped cream is easy yet elegant.
—*Judy Spencer, San Diego, CA*

....

PREP: 20 min. + chilling • **MAKES:** 2 servings

- ¼ cup semisweet chocolate chips
- 1 Tbsp. water
- 1 large egg yolk, lightly beaten
- 1½ tsp. vanilla extract
- ½ cup heavy whipping cream
- 1 Tbsp. sugar
  Optional: Whipped cream and raspberries

1. In a small saucepan, melt the chocolate chips with water; stir until smooth. Stir a small amount of hot chocolate mixture into egg yolk; return all to the pan, stirring constantly. Cook and stir for 2 minutes or until slightly thickened. Remove from heat; stir in the vanilla. Quickly transfer to a small bowl. Stir occasionally until completely cooled.
2. In a small bowl, beat whipping cream until it begins to thicken. Add sugar; beat until soft peaks form. Fold into cooled chocolate mixture. Cover and refrigerate for at least 2 hours. If desired, garnish with whipped cream and raspberries.
1 CUP 367 cal., 31g fat (18g sat. fat), 188mg chol., 29mg sod., 21g carb. (20g sugars, 1g fiber), 3g pro.

CHILLY SNOW DAY FLOATS

When icy flakes are falling and you're cooped up at home, treat yourself to these minty, frothy floats. Feel free to use cream soda in place of lemon-lime—they both work well with the peppermint ice cream.
—*Julianne Schnuck, Milwaukee, WI*

TAKES: 10 min. • **MAKES:** 2 servings

½ cup lemon-lime soda
1 cup peppermint ice cream
½ cup whipped cream
Peppermint candy, optional

Pour the lemon-lime soda into 2 glasses; add the peppermint ice cream. Top with whipped cream. If desired, sprinkle with peppermint candy. Serve immediately with straws and spoons.

1 FLOAT 248 cal., 15g fat (9g sat. fat), 44mg chol., 59mg sod., 27g carb. (19g sugars, 0 fiber), 3g pro.

TEST KITCHEN TIP

Make a cute sled garnish for each soda by aligning 2 candy canes side by side, curved sides up, leaving ½ in. between them, and spreading a little decorating icing on the straight part of canes. Place a graham cracker over icing to resemble a sled, pressing gently to adhere. Allow icing to set for 5 minutes; top cracker with a Sour Patch Kid. Repeat for second soda. For a festive touch, hang sleds off the glasses.

INDIVIDUAL FLANS

INDIVIDUAL FLANS

As an empty nester who loves dessert, I'm always on the lookout for recipes that will deliciously satisfy yet suit our small household. This custard is smooth, rich and just right for my husband and me!
—*Lee Bremson, Kansas City, MO*

TAKES: 30 min. • **MAKES:** 2 servings

2 Tbsp. sweetened shredded coconut
2 tsp. caramel ice cream topping
1 large egg
1 large egg yolk
¾ cup half-and-half cream
3 Tbsp. sugar
¼ tsp. vanilla extract
Pinch ground allspice

1. Divide coconut between 2 ungreased 6-oz. custard cups. Drizzle with the caramel ice cream topping. In a small bowl, whisk the remaining ingredients; pour into the custard cups.
2. Place a steamer rack inside a large skillet. Pour water into skillet until it comes almost to the top of the rack. Place custard cups on rack. Bring to a boil; cover and steam until a knife inserted 1 in. from the edge comes out clean, 10-12 minutes.
3. Remove cups to a wire rack; let stand 10 minutes. Run a knife around the edge of cup. Unmold flans onto dessert plates; serve warm.

1 FLAN 307 cal., 16g fat (9g sat. fat), 258mg chol., 119mg sod., 30g carb. (28g sugars, 0 fiber), 8g pro.

CHILLY SNOW DAY FLOATS

EASY BERRY CHEESECAKE PARFAITS

This recipe takes everything good about cheesecake and makes it easier. You get the rich creaminess, graham cracker crunch and berry flavor all in a fun single-size portion.
—Taste of Home *Test Kitchen*

TAKES: 15 min. • **MAKES:** 2 servings

- 2 oz. cream cheese, softened
- ⅔ cup marshmallow creme
- ½ cup frozen whipped topping
- 4 Tbsp. graham cracker crumbs
- 1 cup fresh raspberries
- 1 cup fresh blueberries

1. Beat cream cheese and marshmallow creme until blended; fold in the whipped topping.

2. Sprinkle 2 Tbsp. graham cracker crumbs into each of 2 glasses or dessert dishes. Layer each with ½ cup cream cheese mixture, ¼ cup raspberries and ¼ cup blueberries; repeat layers. Refrigerate, covered, until serving.

1 PARFAIT 396 cal., 15g fat (9g sat. fat), 29mg chol., 174mg sod., 54g carb. (39g sugars, 6g fiber), 4g pro.

🍎 PUMPKIN PIE SMOOTHIE

I love pumpkin—not only for its taste but also because it's nutritious—and I wanted to have a quick "pie" I could enjoy anytime. A simple smoothie makes a yummy dessert and a special breakfast, too. I top off my glassful with a sprinkle of granola.
—*Alisa Christensen, Rancho Santa Margarita, CA*

TAKES: 10 min. • **MAKES:** 2 servings

- 1 cup ice cubes
- ½ cup 2% milk
- 2 Tbsp. maple syrup
- 2 tsp. almond butter or peanut butter
- ¼ tsp. ground cinnamon or pumpkin pie spice
- ⅔ cup canned pumpkin
- 1 carton (5.3 oz.) fat-free plain Greek yogurt
- 1 Tbsp. granola

Place the first 7 ingredients in a blender; process until blended. Pour into glasses; top with granola.

1¼ CUPS 197 cal., 5g fat (1g sat. fat), 5mg chol., 79mg sod., 30g carb. (21g sugars, 4g fiber), 12g pro.
DIABETIC EXCHANGES 2 starch, 1 fat.

EASY BERRY CHEESECAKE PARFAITS

MUD PIES

After being inspired by ideas for premade individual pie crusts and ice cream, I came up with my own cool combination. I like that it doesn't require any baking.
—*Cassandra Gourley, Williams, AZ*

TAKES: 10 min. • **MAKES:** 2 servings

⅓ cup Nutella
2 individual graham cracker tart shells
1 cup coffee ice cream
Whipped cream and chocolate-covered coffee beans

Spoon Nutella into tart shells. Top each with ice cream; garnish with whipped cream and coffee beans.

1 SERVING 499 cal., 29g fat (8g sat. fat), 26mg chol., 197mg sod., 59g carb. (47g sugars, 2g fiber), 7g pro.

CHOCOLATE TURTLE CHEESECAKE

I always get compliments when I whip up this indulgent treat. With layers of caramel, chocolate and vanilla, it's an instant classic that few can resist. A small springform pan creates the perfect sharing size.
—*Erin Byrd, Springfield, MO*

PREP: 20 min. • **BAKE:** 20 min. + chilling
MAKES: 2 servings

⅓ cup crushed vanilla wafers (about 10 wafers)
4 tsp. butter, melted
4 oz. cream cheese, softened
2 Tbsp. sugar
½ tsp. vanilla extract
2 Tbsp. beaten egg, room temperature
2 Tbsp. hot fudge ice cream topping, warmed
3 Tbsp. hot caramel ice cream topping

1. In a small bowl, combine the vanilla wafer crumbs and butter. Press onto the bottom and ½ in. up the sides of a greased 4-in. springform pan.
2. In a small bowl, beat the cream cheese, sugar and vanilla until smooth. Add egg; beat on low speed just until combined. Spread half of mixture into crust. Stir fudge topping into the remaining batter; gently spread over cream cheese layer. Place pan on a baking sheet.
3. Bake at 350° until the center is almost set, 20-25 minutes. Cool on a wire rack for 10 minutes. Carefully run a knife around the edge of pan to loosen; cool 1 hour longer.
4. Refrigerate overnight. Remove the sides of the pan. Drizzle caramel topping over cheesecake.

½ CHEESECAKE 554 cal., 34g fat (18g sat. fat), 137mg chol., 462mg sod., 58g carb. (48g sugars, 1g fiber), 7g pro.

CONTEST-WINNING EASY TIRAMISU

Here's a fun use for pudding snack cups!
Sweet little servings of tiramisu, garnished
with vanilla wafers and dusted with cocoa,
end any meal on a high note.
—*Betty Claycomb, Alverton, PA*

TAKES: 10 min. • **MAKES:** 2 servings

- 14 vanilla wafers, divided
- 1 tsp. instant coffee granules
- 2 Tbsp. hot water
- 2 snack-size cups (3½ oz. each)
    vanilla pudding
- ¼ cup whipped topping
- 1 tsp. baking cocoa

1. Set aside 4 vanilla wafers; coarsely crush
the remaining wafers. Divide wafer crumbs
between 2 dessert dishes.

2. In a small bowl, dissolve coffee granules
in hot water. Drizzle over wafer crumbs.
Spoon vanilla pudding into dessert dishes.
Top with whipped topping; sprinkle with
cocoa. Garnish with reserved vanilla wafers.

1 SERVING 267 cal., 9g fat (4g sat. fat), 4mg
chol., 219mg sod., 41g carb. (28g sugars, 1g
fiber), 3g pro.

**CONTEST-WINNING
EASY TIRAMISU**

CHOCOLATE CAYENNE SOUFFLES

This rich souffle holds a tongue-tingling surprise—a subtle kick of heat from a touch of cayenne pepper. You'll love it!
—*Diane Halferty, Corpus Christi, TX*

PREP: 25 min. • **BAKE:** 15 min.
MAKES: 2 servings

- 1 large egg
- 1 tsp. plus 1 Tbsp. butter, divided
- 2 tsp. plus 4 Tbsp. sugar, divided
- 2 Tbsp. all-purpose flour
- ½ cup 2% milk
- 2 oz. semisweet chocolate, chopped
- ⅛ tsp. cayenne pepper
  Dash salt
  Confectioners' sugar

1. Separate egg; let stand at room temperature for 30 minutes. Coat two 6-oz. ramekins with 1 tsp. butter and sprinkle with 2 tsp. sugar. Place ramekins on a baking sheet; set aside.
2. In a small saucepan over medium heat, melt remaining butter.
3. Stir in 2 Tbsp. sugar and the flour until smooth. Gradually whisk in the milk. Bring to a boil, stirring constantly. Cook and stir 1-2 minutes longer or until thickened. Whisk in semisweet chocolate, cayenne pepper and salt until chocolate is melted. Transfer to a small bowl.
4. Stir a small amount of hot mixture into egg yolk; return all to the bowl, stirring constantly. Cool slightly.
5. In another bowl, with clean beaters, beat egg white on medium speed until soft peaks form. Gradually beat in remaining sugar on high until stiff peaks form.
6. With a spatula, stir a fourth of the egg white into chocolate mixture until no white streaks remain. Fold in the remaining egg white until combined. Transfer to prepared ramekins.
7. Bake at 400° for 12-15 minutes or until the tops are puffed and centers appear set. Serve immediately. If desired, dust with confectioners' sugar.
1 SOUFFLE 384 cal., 19g fat (10g sat. fat), 125mg chol., 179mg sod., 50g carb. (42g sugars, 2g fiber), 8g pro.

PINEAPPLE UPSIDE-DOWN CAKE

Tender and moist, these two luscious but lighter cakes taste as special as they look. They're guaranteed to please fans of classic pineapple upside-down cake.
—Taste of Home *Test Kitchen*

PREP: 15 min. • **BAKE:** 20 min.
MAKES: 2 servings

- 4 tsp. butter, melted, divided
- 4 tsp. brown sugar
- 2 canned unsweetened pineapple slices
- 2 maraschino cherries
- ⅓ cup all-purpose flour
- 3 Tbsp. sugar
- ½ tsp. baking powder
- ⅛ tsp. salt
  Dash ground nutmeg
- 3 Tbsp. fat-free milk
- ¼ tsp. vanilla extract

1. Pour ½ tsp. butter into each of two 10-oz. ramekins coated with cooking spray. Sprinkle with the brown sugar. Top with a pineapple slice. Place a cherry in the center of each pineapple slice; set aside.
2. In a small bowl, combine the flour, sugar, baking powder, salt and nutmeg. Beat in the milk, vanilla and remaining butter just until combined. Spoon over pineapple.
3. Bake at 350° for 20-25 minutes or until a toothpick inserted in the center comes out clean. Cool for 5 minutes. Run a knife around the edges of ramekins; invert onto dessert plates. Serve warm.
1 CAKE 290 cal., 8g fat (5g sat. fat), 21mg chol., 318mg sod., 53g carb. (37g sugars, 1g fiber), 3g pro.

BLUEBERRY CAKE
WITH WOJAPI SAUCE

BLUEBERRY CAKE WITH WOJAPI SAUCE

This recipe came from my grandmother. The blueberry sauce is traditional Cherokee and has been passed down for generations.
—Angela "WindDancing" Hatchett, Altoona, AL

....

PREP: 20 min. • **BAKE:** 20 min. + cooling
MAKES: 2 servings

- ¼ **cup sugar**
- ¼ **cup self-rising flour**
- ¼ **cup 2% milk**
- ⅛ **tsp. vanilla extract**
- 1 **Tbsp. butter, melted**
- ¼ **cup fresh or frozen blueberries**

WOJAPI SAUCE
- 2 **Tbsp. sugar**
- 1½ **tsp. cornstarch**
- ¼ **cup water**
- 1 **cup fresh or frozen blueberries**
  Vanilla ice cream, optional

1. Preheat oven to 350°. In a small bowl, combine sugar and flour; stir in milk and vanilla. Place butter in a greased 5¾x3x2-in. loaf pan. Pour batter into pan (do not stir). Sprinkle with blueberries.

2. Bake until a toothpick inserted in the center comes out clean, 20-25 minutes. Cool for 10 minutes before inverting onto a serving plate.

3. In a small saucepan combine sugar and cornstarch. Stir in water until smooth; add blueberries. Bring to a boil. Reduce heat; cook and stir until thickened, 1-2 minutes. Serve warm over cake with vanilla ice cream if desired.

1 PIECE 323 cal., 7g fat (4g sat. fat), 18mg chol., 234mg sod., 65g carb. (48g sugars, 2g fiber), 3g pro.

CHOCOLATE LAVA CAKES

While you enjoy your main course, let two decadent chocolate cakes bake for dessert. They're best enjoyed while still oven-warm.
—Heidi Wilcox, Lapeer, MI

....

TAKES: 25 min. • **MAKES:** 2 servings

- ⅓ **cup semisweet chocolate chips**
- ¼ **cup butter, cubed**
- ⅓ **cup superfine sugar**
- 1 **large egg, room temperature**
- 4½ **tsp. all-purpose flour**
- ¼ **cup white baking chips**
  Confectioners' sugar

1. Grease the bottom and sides of two 6-oz. ramekins or custard cups. Place ramekins on a baking sheet; set aside.

2. In a microwave, melt the semisweet chocolate and butter; stir until smooth. Set aside to cool.

3. In a small bowl, combine sugar, egg and flour; stir in chocolate mixture. Fold in white baking chips. Spoon batter into prepared ramekins.

4. Bake at 400° until a thermometer reads 160° and the sides of the cakes are set, 15-20 minutes. Remove ramekins to a wire rack to cool for 5 minutes. Invert the cakes onto serving plates; dust with confectioners' sugar.

1 CAKE 635 cal., 40g fat (24g sat. fat), 169mg chol., 219mg sod., 68g carb. (61g sugars, 2g fiber), 6g pro.

CREAMY BUTTERSCOTCH PUDDING

One day when I had a craving for something homemade, I tried from-scratch pudding. It's much better than the store-bought kind!
—*EMR, Taste of Home Online Community*

PREP: 10 min. • **COOK:** 10 min. + chilling
MAKES: 2 servings

- ¼ cup packed brown sugar
- 1 Tbsp. plus 1 tsp. cornstarch
  Dash salt
- 1 cup fat-free milk
- 1 large egg yolk, lightly beaten
- 1½ tsp. butter
- ¾ tsp. vanilla extract
- 2 Pirouette cookies, optional

1. In a small saucepan, combine the brown sugar, cornstarch and salt. Add the milk and egg yolk; stir until smooth. Cook and stir over medium heat until the mixture comes to a boil. Cook and stir until thickened, 1-2 minutes longer.

2. Remove from the heat; stir in butter and vanilla. Cool to room temperature, stirring several times. Pour into 2 individual dessert dishes. Cover and refrigerate until chilled, 1-2 hours. If desired, serve with Pirouette cookies.

½ CUP 217 cal., 5g fat (2g sat. fat), 111mg chol., 157mg sod., 38g carb. (33g sugars, 0 fiber), 5g pro.

CREAMY BUTTERSCOTCH PUDDING

WARM PINEAPPLE SUNDAES WITH RUM SAUCE

Fresh pineapple, rum and brown sugar make a dreamy flavor combination. Adding ginger and butter takes this treat to another level.
—*Jamie Miller, Maple Grove, MN*

TAKES: 25 min. • **MAKES:** 2 servings

- 4 fresh pineapple spears (about 8 oz.)
- ½ cup packed brown sugar
- 2 Tbsp. dark rum
- ¾ tsp. ground ginger
- 4 tsp. butter, cut into small pieces
- 2 scoops vanilla ice cream or low-fat frozen yogurt
- 4 gingersnap cookies, crushed

1. Place the pineapple in a 1-qt. baking dish. In a small bowl, combine the brown sugar, rum and ginger; spoon over the pineapple. Dot with butter.

2. Bake, uncovered, at 425° until pineapple is lightly browned and sauce is bubbly, 8-10 minutes. Place ice cream in 2 dessert dishes; top with pineapple and sauce. Serve immediately with crushed cookies.

1 SERVING 536 cal., 16g fat (10g sat. fat), 49mg chol., 221mg sod., 95g carb. (78g sugars, 2g fiber), 4g pro.

RECIPE INDEX